One of Us

One of Us

BY
Diane Glancy

WIPF & STOCK · Eugene, Oregon

ONE OF US

Copyright © 2015 Diane Glancy. All rights reserved. Except for brief quotations in critical publications or reviews, no part of this book may be reproduced in any manner without prior written permission from the publisher. Write: Permissions, Wipf and Stock Publishers, 199 W. 8th Ave., Suite 3, Eugene, OR 97401.

Wipf & Stock
An Imprint of Wipf and Stock Publishers
199 W. 8th Ave., Suite 3
Eugene, OR 97401

www.wipfandstock.com

ISBN 13: 978-1-62564-704-7

Manufactured in the U.S.A.   01/22/2015

…we strive only for a closely invested brand of verisimilitude.
—T. C. Boyle, *The Women*

There's an imagination around events.
—E. L. Doctorow, discussing *Homer and Langley* on *Charlie Rose*

Faustus. I think hell's a fable.
Mephistopheles. Ay, think so still,
till experience change thy mind.
—Christopher Marlowe, *Dr. Faustus*

Contents

Introduction | xi

1. Mark Cabot: Senior Pastor, Christ Church | 1
2. Ralph Gheary: Assistant Pastor | 4
3. Zelda Gheary: The Interruption | 6
4. Ralph Gheary: It Ran Together | 8
5. Zelda Gheary: Alone | 9
6. Mark Cabot: A Christian Manual of War | 11
7. Zelda Gheary: Flannel Graph | 13
8. Ralph Gheary: Unbelievable | 14
9. Zelda Gheary: The Yellow Christ | 15
10. Mark Cabot: A Call | 16
11. Ralph Gheary: The Day We Sat Stunned | 18
12. Mark Cabot: A Meeting with Thomas Fout | 20
13. Zelda Gheary: Flannel Graph Again | 24
14. Thomas Fout: Requiem | 25
15. Zelda Gheary: The Hearing | 26
16. Mark Cabot: The Saiths' Cabin | 28
17. Ralph Gheary: Confrontation | 34
18. Mark Cabot: The Sermon | 35
19. Zelda Gheary: The Drawing | 38
20. Mark Cabot: In Those Desperate Days | 40
21. Zelda Gheary: Subworld | 41

22	Ralph Gheary: Holding Back the Flood	43
23	Zelda Gheary: I Had to Have Something to Do	44
24	The Demons: The Gloat	46
25	Zelda Gheary: Another Hearing	47
26	Ralph Gheary: The Tin Man	49
27	Zelda Gheary: History of Art	50
28	Ralph Gheary: So Much for the Poverty in the World	55
29	Zelda Gheary: The Stunned Christ	58
30	Mark Cabot: There Would Be No Escape	61
31	Zelda Gheary: Where Do You Go When the Vultures Fly?	67
32	Mark Cabot: Mephistopheles Himself	72
33	Zelda Gheary: A Prayer for Ruth Fout	76
34	Mark Cabot: Rhododendrons	78
35	Zelda Gheary: The Ceiling	81
36	Mark Cabot: The Ministry	82
37	Ralph Gheary: A Visit with Thomas Fout	85
38	Zelda Gheary: Upper Room	88
39	Grace Cabot: The Pastor's Wife	89
40	Zelda Gheary: Zelda Leads Women's Prayer	90
41	Mark Cabot: A Snake at the Saiths' Cabin	92
42	Ralph Gheary: Anger	97
43	Zelda Gheary: The E-mails	99
44	Ralph Gheary: Another Trip to Jail	101
45	Zelda Gheary: Forth Worth Museum	102
46	Grace Cabot: Church Supper	105
47	Mark Cabot: The Struggle with Sin	111
48	Ralph Gheary: Free Will	114
49	Mark Cabot: Several Visits	115
50	Ralph Gheary: The Sentencing	117
51	Mark Cabot: A Prayer to Wash the Church	118
52	Zelda Gheary: Swallow a Camel	120

53 Mark Cabot: District Meeting of Ministers | 121
54 Zelda Gheary: A Recurring Dream | 126
55 Grace Cabot: Daughters | 127
56 Mark Cabot: The Saiths' | 130
57 Ralph Gheary: Get Him off My Mind | 132
58 Mark Cabot: The Church Election | 134
59 Grace Cabot: A Consideration | 136
60 Mark Cabot: Grace Cabot's Breakdown | 137
61 Grace Cabot: McPherson | 141
62 Zelda Gheary: Now the Drawings Have Voices | 143
63 Mark Cabot: Separation | 144
64 Zelda Gheary: Covered Dishes | 147
65 Grace Cabot: Tessa | 148
66 Mark Cabot: I Woke Trembling One Morning | 151
67 Zelda Gheary: Soot | 154
68 Mark Cabot: Mark Retrieves His Wife and Daughter | 156
69 Ralph Gheary: His Sermon | 158
70 Mark Cabot: Trouble Within | 161
71 Ralph Gheary: A Call | 163
72 Mark Cabot: Exorcism | 164
73 Ralph Gheary: The Unpardonable Sin | 167
74 Zelda Gheary: The Installation | 170
75 Mark Cabot: There Were Other Murders in Kansas | 171
76 Grace Cabot: A Visit with Ruth Fout | 176
77 Mark Cabot: The Saiths' Cabin by Themselves | 178
78 Zelda Gheary: What a Little Box | 181
79 Mark Cabot: Fout | 182
80 Zelda Gheary: The Lock | 188
81 Mark Cabot: The Bookshelf | 189
82 Ralph Gheary: Bicycle | 194
83 Mark Cabot: The Struggle with Sin | 195

84 Grace Cabot: A Reminder | 197
85 Mark Cabot: A Little Wind Blows in Kansas | 198
86 Ralph Gheary: What's in the Locked Room? | 201
87 Zelda Gheary: Aftermath | 203
88 Mark Cabot: Night Was the Worst | 204
89 Zelda Gheary: Places We Should Not Go | 208
90 Ralph Gheary: Calculation | 209
91 Mark Cabot: Reconciliation | 210
92 Thomas Fout: Save Me, O God | 215
93 Mark Cabot: Tessa Again | 217
94 Zelda Gheary: City of Refuge | 219
95 Mark Cabot: But for the Accident | 221

Introduction

Mention Jesus, and some people want to leave the room. Mention a church in Kansas where a man who was president of the congregation murdered ten people, and the people might stay.

I was in Richmond, Kentucky, on the weekend of February 25, 2005, when CNN announced the arrest of the man who called himself "BTK": Bind, Torture, Kill. When I saw Reverend Michael Clark, the pastor of Christ Lutheran Church in Wichita, standing before news reporters, stunned that BTK was a member of his congregation, the questions appeared: How does a minister deal with a murderer in his own congregation? What is the nature of evil? What is our resilience to it? How far can a Christian go and still be a Christian? What is the definition of a Christian? Why Christianity?

I have written as an outsider to the event. I am interested in a work of imagination for the purpose of exploring issues. I used the arrest of BTK as the triggering event. The method of arrest—a disk from the church computer—and the murder of ten people are the same, but the story is its own.

In the process of writing, I found the story slicing between the voices of Mark and Grace Cabot, the minister of Christ Church and his wife, as well as the voices of Ralph and Zelda Gheary, the youth and assistant minister and his wife. Everyone wanted a turn, trying to speak before the others. Twice I let Thomas Fout, the murderer, speak. And once, the demons.

1

Mark Cabot
Senior Pastor, Christ Church

I was at my desk with my sermon notes when the church secretary opened my office door without knocking. I had heard a car drive up, but hadn't paid attention. Three men stood before me. The door remained open. I knew they were authorities of some sort. I stood, confused. They had a disk from a computer they thought belonged to the church. They had questions. Who had the disk belonged to? Who made the list of church duties?

"It looks like one of our discs, but they're standard—"

Other men came into the secretary's office and unplugged the computer. They would have to take it with them. They unplugged mine also. I saw there was a van in the church drive as well as the sheriff's car. Was the church under arrest?

"Who used the computer for this list?" the men asked.

I recognized the duties immediately. I gave them his name. They finished packing the equipment they needed and left.

I called Grace, my wife, and told her something was up, but I didn't know what. The men had asked that I not say anything.

The authorities returned. I saw they were from federal as well as state agencies. How well did I know Thomas Fout?

"I've been his pastor several years. He was here when I came."

"Did he have access to the church computers?"

"Yes."

They said they were certain that Thomas Fout was the man who had murdered ten people over a period of years.

My secretary wept in a way I had not seen her weep in all the years I had known her, not even at the death of her parents.

I called the bishop when the authorities left.

I called my wife again on her cell phone. I told her not to answer questions—not to let anyone in the house. Not to say anything on the phone. She wasn't home anyway, she said.

I asked about our daughter.

"Clare's at school, of course, then she's going to a friend's house."

I drove to the Fouts' place. The street was blocked. I'd never seen more state and city vehicles. Reporters and camera vans continued to arrive. People gathered outside the crime-scene tape that blocked off the street. I could show them I was a pastor. The Fouts' pastor. I could get through. But I backed away.

I returned to the church and closed the door of my office to pray, but I was soon interrupted with calls. One of them was my friend and a member of my congregation, Roy Saith. I asked him to stay with Grace and Clare when they got home. Already there were calls from church members. Was it true? Yes. How could it be true? I didn't know. I told my secretary to leave a message on the answering machine that I would meet with reporters after the authorities made their official announcement. I told her to call Ralph Gheary, the youth minister who also served as my assistant. He was in Elwood at the funeral of his wife's grandmother. Then I told my secretary to go home.

The announcement was televised the next day. I knew Ralph had returned without Zelda, but now she was with him. Families of the victims sat in the courthouse to hear that at last the murderer of their relatives had been caught. At last, the police and agents were sure. They had felt sure the last time they arrested someone. But now they were sure again. This time they had DNA evidence.

Mark Cabot: Senior Pastor, Christ Church

The bishop arrived that evening. We would meet the reporters at the church tomorrow afternoon.

Grace seemed to be holding up.

I called Ruth Fout all evening until I got through. A man answered, a relative I didn't know. The family was gathering. A brother had been called from Iraq. Would they like for me to come to the house? No, Ruth was resting in her room. A doctor had been to the house to see her.

2

Ralph Gheary
Assistant Pastor

We were at the gate of the cemetery when my cell phone rang. It was Christ Church in Buckholt, Kansas, where I was assistant minister. Thomas Fout had been arrested. A member of our church had been arrested for murder. Multiple murders. A murderer who had been—who still was—president of the congregation of Christ Church. What was it that I felt? Disbelief? No, I knew immediately. It was anger over the interruption in the way I planned my ministry.

We followed the hearse into the Elwood, Kansas, cemetery for the internment of my wife's grandmother. I held the cell phone so Zelda could hear. I didn't know what to say, other than to give voice to my disbelief. Anger would come to Zelda also, I knew already. Was this a trick of God on us—this leading us to a church that lodged a murderer? I felt betrayed. Just a few months ago, we had arrived at Christ Church in Buckholt to begin our lives together as the new assistant pastor and his new wife.

"It can't be—" I tried to speak, but words didn't come. I blurted something—I can't believe . . . Are they sure? No, it's not true. But it was.

We had known about the murders for years. Everyone in Kansas had. But to have the murderer in our own congregation?

"I have to go back this afternoon," I said.

"Do you want to get out of the car right now?" Zelda asked, angered at the interruption of her grandmother's funeral.

"I'll need the car," I said.

Ralph Gheary: Assistant Pastor

"I'm not through with my grandmother's funeral. I don't want this intrusion."

"Neither do I. But it's here. You can stay as long as you want. Call me when you want to come back."

3

Zelda Gheary
The Interruption

We stopped behind the cars that carried my parents, my brothers, and their families. I saw the back doors of the hearse already open. I never had felt such swift anger. Who was this man to tear up our lives? I could murder him. Was I as guilty in God's sight as Thomas Fout? Hardly.

"I'm sorry, Zelda—"

"Mark didn't even call you, but his secretary."

Ralph didn't answer. Why did I feel the need to wound him?

We got out of the car. The wind flapped the large canopy that had been placed over the gravesite. My brothers and other family members carried my grandmother's casket to the open grave. I was aware of the silence in the cemetery, except for the birds and the flapping of the canopy edge back upon itself in the wind. The usher talked in a low voice, directing us where to sit.

"Here," my mother called me to her side in the front row of chairs.

I hadn't expected to be a minister's wife. I wanted to be an artist. But I found it was beyond my ability. My mother had taken me to art lessons at the library when I was a child. I loved the way one color swirled into the other, changing both of them into something they had not been by themselves. It was the way I thought about marriage.

I hardly listened to the minister as he spoke. I was thinking about Thomas Fout, who had brought murder into the church. I would have to find a way to understand this travesty. Maybe I could use art to see murder and unfairness too. Maybe it hadn't happened after all. I felt my mother tug at my hand. I had to remember I was at my grandmother's funeral.

My grandmother, Griselda Foster, had outlived her husband and her friends. Her funeral was family, our friends in Elwood, and a several churchwomen who came to anything that happened at the church, even funerals.

Now there were a few last words at the graveside. The minister prayed. Friends passed before us with their condolences. I took a flower from the bouquet on my grandmother's casket and followed Ralph to our car.

"I'll ride with my parents," I told him.

He leaned forward to kiss me on the cheek, but I turned my head.

He left after saying goodbye to my family.

"What happened?" my father asked.

"A man in our church was arrested."

"What for?"

"Murder."

4

Ralph Gheary
It Ran Together

It all ran together. A man had been arrested. The man was a member of our church. Zelda and I had sat beside him and his wife. What was she going through? He was president of the congregation. A Boy Scout leader. A pillar. I struggled to hold the funeral and the arrest apart. The flat country, the placid fields, the grazing cattle, the gravel driveways into farmyards, the fences and hedgerows passed at a steady pace as I returned to Buckholt.

We'd hardly been a day in Elwood. Zelda's grandmother had died in her sleep. There was visitation at the church the night we arrived, and then the funeral the next day. This day. Why did I suddenly feel I was in another time? I didn't want to leave Elwood. I wanted to be with Zelda. At the same time, I had to watch my speed as I traveled.

5

Zelda Gheary
Alone

"Where's Ralph going?" my brother asked. Both of my brothers stood together. I saw their reddish brown hair and straight noses, a trait of the Foster family. In the sun, I saw my older brother's hair was marked with gray. His skin seemed dry, and for the first time, I saw wrinkles in his face.

"A man in our congregation is the murderer of all those people in Buckholt years ago," I said. I wanted to get in the car, away from the wind, but the little group of people stood around us, talking.

I knew when I married into the ministry that there would be times when the church came first. There would be events to deal with that took precedence.

Neighbors brought food to my grandmother's house that evening. After the meal, a niece followed me to the porch. We sat on the swing in our coats as shadows came across my grandmother's yard. Once in a while I looked down the road in the direction Ralph had gone.

I never thought, newly married, I would be alone. Why hadn't I gone with him? Had I made a mistake? Why had I chosen to stay with my family? Wasn't Ralph my family now? But I wanted to be in Elwood with the memory of my grandmother. I wanted time to grieve. Thomas Fout was not going to take that from me.

That evening, my first away from Ralph since we married, he called on my cell phone. I got my coat and went to the porch. The church was stunned. Buckholt was stunned. The country, even. Reporters and vans and cameras were arriving at the church. No, I hadn't seen the news. We were upstairs deciding what to do with my grandmother's possessions. I saw my brothers through the front window. They were watching the news on television. I didn't want to look yet. I would hear enough of it. I apologized to Ralph for my rudeness in the car. I stood in a corner of the front porch and listened to his voice. My niece watched me from the front window.

Ralph called again the next day and said there would be an official announcement of Fout's arrest at the courthouse the next morning. Could I be there with him and our other church members?

"It's a four-hour trip," I told Ralph on the phone, "My aunts are here to sort through my grandmother's belongings. We're already in the attic."

"I made it in three," he said. "I think we both should be here to support the church."

I didn't say anything for a moment.

"I don't want to be there without you," he said.

Late that afternoon, my parents drove me to Buckholt and stayed with us through the first week. Ralph rented a bed for them and put it in the second bedroom, where I kept my art supplies.

Fout had lived among us, but we hadn't known him. I mean, I knew him. I knew who he was. He was a spokesman. He greeted us when we came to Christ Church just a few months ago. I shook his hand. I had touched a murderer. I listened to Ralph talk to his friends on the phone. There was something new in his voice. It was an unbelievable quandary to occupy his professors and friends from seminary.

Lord, when you spoke, the flannel graph in Sunday school came alive. I saw the striped robes of your disciples, their feet dusty in their sandals. I saw the desert. The camels and sheep. Don't abandon me. When you spoke, I heard the thunder and lightning when the wind blew down from heaven.

6

Mark Cabot
A Christian Manual of War

We met at the church the next day—the bishop, the men's prayer group, Ralph Gheary, and his wife, Zelda, my wife, Grace, and other members who wanted to pray with us. I locked the front door as news vans and reporters were arriving. I opened the meeting with a Scripture. I placed boundaries upon the floodwaters. They could come so far and no farther.

"You set a bound that they may not pass over; that they turn not again to cover the earth."[1] I held those words. Whatever floodwaters were ahead, they could not cover us. There would be dry places where we could stand. I reminded the troubles ahead of their bounds. They could not cover us. I had not felt this threatened since our daughter Tessa died from meningitis. She was not yet nine. We stood from our prayer. I went to the door of the church and pushed it open. I looked at the news reporters—at the people who had gathered.

I saw the cameras—the microphones in my face. I heard the questions. Thomas Fout was a member of my church? The man arrested for murder? Yes. Yes. He was president of the congregation. He was an ordinance officer in his community. Did I know it was the church that led authorities to Thomas Fout? No, not at first. But yes, I knew it now. Fout had used the church computer to send a note to the newspaper. They had written an article asking what happened to the man who had committed so many

---

1. Ps 104:8–9.

murders. It had been twenty-five years since his last crime. Had he disappeared? Had he died? Fout sent the disk saying he had not left the area, erasing a list of his church duties from the disk before he wrote the note. The investigators retrieved the erased words on the disk. They traced it to the church. I, the pastor, had identified the man whose list it was.

Had I seen him yet? the reporters asked. No, I hadn't seen him yet, but I was going to meet with him soon. He had asked to see his pastor. Had I seen his family? Yes. I talked with them on the phone. Had his wife known? No. She was distraught. How could she have not known? She didn't know.

I stood on Scripture. It was what held me up that day. I kept hearing my own questions: Had the church brought him down? Was it God who expelled him from the church and said that this man must pay for his crimes?

I had stood before the reporters. Yes, Thomas Fout was a member of my church. Not someone I saw once a year, but someone who was a part of my congregation. He was a leader of the congregation. He walked into church whenever he wanted. He had access to the office. To the computer. How could a man have been both murderer and member of my congregation? How could he have been an ordinance officer in Buckholt, yet broken the law himself?

Reporters and more reporters came like water. We continued to pray in my office for strength. We went out to meet them again. The bishop stood with me. I was caught with a murderer in my pocket. A wolf in my flock of sheep. Why had Fout not risen up on a Sunday morning and taken our lives? What moved in Fout's mind as he sang hymns? As he listened to sermons? My sermons? And the former pastor's. How freakish. He heard a sermon and went out and murdered. How could I live that down? Why was I thinking about myself? My secretary had been alone with him in the church. She had been at risk and not known it. She had been in danger.

There was relief that the murderer was caught. He would not kill again. It had been twenty-five years since his last act. Now the mystery was solved. But the relief was tempered with horror.

Thomas Fout had brought us to the knowledge of what we didn't want. He was not separate from us. He was one of us.

7

Zelda Gheary
Flannel Graph

I had been an art major in college. I offered to make Biblical characters for the flannel graphs at church. I didn't realize it would set the Sunday school teachers on edge. I withdrew my offer. Now I could make a murderer for their new lesson on the flannel board.

8

Ralph Gheary
Unbelievable

It was unbelievable. A second catastrophe. No—not as bad. But how many could we bear? A dog was hit. The car swerved and ran off the road in front of our church. No one was hurt, except the dog. But the police cars were at the church again. Passers-by slowed and looked. Trouble at that church again? What have they done now? I stood in the parking lot with the upset driver until Animal Control came for the body of the dog.

9

Zelda Gheary
The Yellow Christ

I would handle my anger the way I usually did. I would get out one of my art books.

"If you knew art history, you wouldn't feel isolated—" I told Ralph.

I opened the book at Paul Gauguin's "The Yellow Christ." 1889. "Look at Jesus on the cross—his uninterested face. His elongated body. The flattened space. The rustic primitiveness of the painting. The grotesqueness of it. He was part of the Symbolist movement. Gauguin—not Christ. Everything stood for something else. Look at the man in the background, climbing away from him over the wall. Is that you, Ralph?"

"There are things art can't handle, Zelda," Ralph said.

10

Mark Cabot
A Call

I knew I had to call the previous minister. I sat at my desk a long time before I called.

"Reverend Cole? Mark Cabot."

"Yes, Mark, how are you?"

"I wanted you to know there's trouble at the church. I want you to know in case you're contacted. Thomas Fout has been arrested. It turns out he's the man who committed all those murders that plagued Buckholt some years back."

There was a prolonged silence—

"Reverend Cole—?"

"There must be a mistake," he interrupted, almost angrily. "Tom couldn't be the one."

"He is. Beyond a doubt. DNA evidence. It is certain."

There was another period of silence.

I thought of what I could say to ease the news. But there wasn't anything I could say other than the facts.

Reverend Cole's voice was unsteady. He seemed to stammer a moment.

"It can't be."

"It is. Turn on the news."

"Ruth Fout and the children?"

He seemed to cough, and I knew he was struggling for his calm, ministerial voice.

Mark Cabot: A Call

"This is a shock. I don't know what to say. I don't think Thomas is capable of murder. He's a—" Cole paused.

"A leader in the church," I said. "Yes, he is. Or was. He is now in jail."

I heard Reverend Cole groan under the weight of the news. He was old. Retired. He thought he was in green pastures.

"What can I do?"

"Pray for us."

"Certainly."

"I will keep you posted."

It was an awkward conversation. There would be a lot more of them ahead.

I stepped out of my office. How could I get any work done? Mildred Keller, the secretary, was on the phone. Grace, my wife, was there too, helping Mildred with the calls. Technicians were returning our computers and some of our equipment. At least now, we could receive and return e-mails. I talked to another reporter who came to the church. I had a call from jail. Thomas Fout requested a visit.

11

Ralph Gheary
The Day We Sat Stunned

There were gawkers on Sunday morning—people we had not seen before. There were sounds of open sobs in the congregation. I watched Mark Cabot from a chair beside the pulpit. I wanted to see how he would get through the service. If he couldn't do it, I felt I could step up. Zelda sat in the front row with her parents. I saw her wipe her eyes as Mark spoke. What I remember of Mark Cabot's sermon after Fout's arrest: This is the question. Can a murderer enter heaven? The answer is no. No murderer has eternal life.[1] Yet Moses murdered.[2] He's in heaven. Surely he came with Elijah and was seen on the Mount of Transfiguration by Jesus and his disciples, Peter, James, and John.[3] David murdered. Not directly, but he ordered Uriah, the husband of Bathsheba, on the front line of battle so he would be killed.[4] Yet Jesus is the root and offspring of David.[5] These are the contradictions we face. These are the difficulties of Scripture.

I talked to the youth at our regular meeting on Sunday evenings.

1. 1 John 3:15.
2. Exod 2:12.
3. Matt 17:3.
4. 2 Sam 11:15.
5. Rev 22:16.

Ralph Gheary: The Day We Sat Stunned

"The leader of our congregation has murdered ten people. He has broken into houses, devastated the lives of the people who lived there."

Zelda sat beside me as I spoke. I worried that she might cry. I watched the faces of the group, looking at Zelda, looking away from her, or both, mainly to avoid looking at each other. They were wondering how to face their friends at school who knew they belonged to the church where a murderer had been arrested. They would be teased. Ridiculed for their church attendance. It was an awkward meeting. All of us were discouraged. "Defeated" was probably the better word. I finally closed with a prayer and we left silently, except for the few encouragements we could give.

12

Mark Cabot
A Meeting with Thomas Fout

I went to the jail and met with Thomas Fout, the member of my congregation. He was in trouble. He wanted prayer. He wanted consideration. He sat behind a table in an orange inmate suit when I walked in the room. I was awkward. I bumped my leg on the edge of the table as I sat down across from him. We looked at one another. Was it fear I felt? Who would speak first? We were waiting for the current to break—we were snagged. What was I trying to do? Why hadn't I prepared myself? But how?

We were not strangers, but the meeting was the stranger between us. The room in which we sat could have been on another planet. He had been caught. I was caught with him. I did not want to be here. He did not want to be here either, now that the officers were gone and he was no longer the center of their attention. Now that he could not leave the building, let alone the room. I didn't want to be here, but as I looked at him, I wasn't sure he didn't, if he could be here on his own terms. It almost seemed that he had the authority and I was the recipient of his visit. He was the pastor in a perverse way. I had come for instruction for my ignorance. How could I meet this situation in which I was a stranger? I remembered people who had come to the church for help—who had sat in my office, overwhelmed.

"Should we pray?" I asked then, without waiting for his answer, because I realized it was my place as the pastor to decide. I bowed my head and began, "Lord, be with us. We come to you for guidance." I'm not sure what else I said.

"I understand you're the one who turned me in," Tom said.

"The authorities asked who wrote a list," I told him, "I answered them." I was not going to allow him to have the upper hand. I was not here to defend myself.

Tom said he had met with investigators. He had felt camaraderie. They all were corrections officers—he and they. He had confessed. Then the investigators were gone, and he was alone. He was devastated. They had had an understanding. Then they abandoned him. Now he was an inmate. Now he was alone. He had sent a disk to the newspaper. He had asked if the erased files on a disk could be resurrected. That wasn't the word he used—"retrieved," I suppose. Or "recovered." They said no. He sent the disk with more information about his murders. They found the erased files of his church duties. Thomas must have known. He wanted to be caught. Not convicted of his crimes and left alone. But he wanted attention.

I was aware how tightly I held my shoulders as I talked—as I listened—as I thought—as I tried to reconcile—to resolve—to understand the horrific details that were disclosed.

Thomas Fout felt betrayed. He felt hurt. He saw the murders as accomplishments. He thought the investigators wanted to talk to him, be involved with him as he led them on an adventure. They would be impressed with his skill. He thought they would remain in contact with him, not leave alone him in his cell. I was stunned. I tried not to show it. I had never seen him think this way.

I gave Fout what I could. I had to be honest.

There were awkward moments of silence. Did he see my nervousness? There were awkward moments of us speaking over one another, of interrupting without meaning to. You first—No, you—Go ahead. We were fishing. We were casting reels. We were not standing in the same stream. Had I seen his wife? Had his children come to Buckholt? Where were his brothers? The rest of his family?

How could I resolve what could not be resolved? It had torn our community—it had cut me—I didn't want to see Thomas Fout. I wanted to leap from my chair, from this room, from this place, and flee. I couldn't get far enough away if I drove for the rest of my life. The land was tainted with his acts of murder. The place itself wanted to flee from him, from what he did. I felt sick to my stomach. I felt sick in my spirit. I felt touched with a filth

One of Us

I couldn't wash off. What else could I say? There were cities of refuge in the Old Testament for murderers, but those were accidental murders. Not planned and executed with precision.

"You carried a kit with tape and rope—"

"I want forgiveness," Tom said.

"That's between you and God. I can't think that far yet. I can't even think about what you've done. You've implicated the church also. God's salvation is irrevocable. Christ may be your city of refuge. He may accept you in his mercy. I can say, God forgives you. But right now, I, myself, cannot."

My head hurt. My shoulders were stiff. I was shaking. Did he see my shudders? Did he see my weakness? I could hardly get up from my chair. I felt like I was a stone. A huge, numb, cold, angry piece of rock. He would have kept me longer. He would have kept me prisoner. But I had to leave the room. I had to get out before I fell there.

I thought about Thomas Fout on the way home from the jail. I knew I would think of nothing else for days to come—months—even years. How would I maneuver my way through whatever was ahead? How could I steer my family and congregation through what had happened? What exactly had happened? How could I understand? Didn't God control the events in our lives? Isn't that what we learned from the book of Job? Was God in this at all?

God was a murderer—of animals, certainly, for skins to clothe Adam and Eve—and all the blood sacrifices God required in the Old Testament. How many times did he call down fire on his rebellious people? Moses pleaded with him more than once for leniency. How many times did God command Israel to kill their enemies, every man, woman, infant, suckling, ox, camel, sheep, and ass?[1] It was so Israel would not be perverted by other gods and customs. It was for their own good, I tried to rationalize. God killed his own Son on the cross—it was necessary for the salvation of man—in the Christians' opinion, anyway. God had to judge sin. Jesus became sin on the cross. He was judged and suffered death. Jesus rose again. God's judgment on sin was satisfied. That was the crux of the Christian religion—for most Christians, anyway. I was aware of unbelief. I was aware of the many who thought the Bible was irrelevant, or tried to warp it to say something that almost looked like the message of the Bible, or made a spirituality of their

---

1. 1 Sam 15:3.

own construction. I was aware of the theories that tried to discredit—to undermine—what for me was fact. If we believed Christ died on the cross and was raised, we were raised with him, our sins forgiven. What was so hard about that?

13

Zelda Gheary
Flannel Graph Again

I heard the Bible all my life. Sunday school attendance came with flannel graphs and Biblical characters parting the Red Sea and standing beside a horrific burning bush. There were no flannel graphs to explain how a man could murder and sit in church in the next day. There were no flannel graphs of the Hebrews in the wilderness—the battle of Edrei, for instance, when they fought an enemy tribe until none of the other tribe remained. Neither were there flannel graphs of the Hebrew massacre of the enemy tribes in the promised land. That was our God. And it was good to be on his side. There wasn't much hope otherwise. I wouldn't say I was held to the gospel by fear of hell. But I could visualize what it looked like.

The flannel board brought me to Sunday school. If there were a fire, I would have run for the board and carried it from the burning church.

14

Thomas Fout
Requiem

I had something turned on now. It always had been there. My friend—the executioner. Did I want to follow? Did I want to provide involvement? I felt the precision if it. The lifting into *mission*. Into *project*. This gallant roaming going farther all the time. Yes. *Yes*—I thought my way through it. I decided how I would go. That was what was terrifying to them—how easy it was to murder. How natural it seemed.

15

Zelda Gheary
The Hearing

I sat next to Ralph during the hearing. My parents were several rows behind us. I had the feeling nothing was real. I saw Thomas Fout in a white suit sitting at a table ahead of us. I trembled in disgust. I felt myself floating away from the courtroom. I thought of my grandmother. I thought of my art books. Whatever happened, the visual representation of paint on canvas would hold what had to be held steady. It was a certainty. If I looked at Giotto's "Christ Entering Jerusalem," with its pastel robes and angels climbing into the sky, then its purpose and symmetry would shift into my life. I believed in Christianity. But the certainty of order in God's world was shaken. There was a rip in the canvas. Something was there that wasn't supposed to happen. I was someplace I hadn't been. As a child, I had slept at my grandmother's house. It was my first outing away from my parents and brothers. In her house, the curtains moved in the breeze with their pastel robes. I felt myself trembling. I saw the ceiling move. I couldn't tell anyone. Only the ceiling and I knew. I felt Ralph's arm around me—pulling me—pulling me back from the air.

People looked at us as we walked from the courtroom after the hearing. Ralph walked past news reporters and would not answer. I saw one of them had cornered Mark Cabot. That evening, my mother and I fixed supper while Ralph and my father watched television. There were interviews with neighbors and anyone else who had known Thomas Fout, or thought they had known him. The same information over and over. I felt the rise of anger I could push into a ball and hide somewhere inside me. My parents' quiet tolerance was something solid I could feel.

16

Mark Cabot
The Saiths' Cabin

The sky above us was smeared with moonlight. I carried our luggage into the cabin. My wife, Grace, would unpack it. Our daughter, Clare, was already drawn up under a blanket in front of the television. I came sometimes to Orbson Lake to work. Ralph Gheary, the youth pastor, would be at the church. It was not my cabin, but my friend Roy Saith's. I liked the feel of being a tenant. That's what I was on the earth. I didn't want to get comfortable, to sit back and feel I had accomplished what I needed to accomplish. To say, "This is mine."

I had come to the cabin to get away from the calls, to think, to write a sermon that would reach out to my stunned congregation. To say what I could. To answer. To get my footing. What could I say, other than the stammerings I made after Fout's arrest? A member of my congregation had murdered ten people. Thomas Fout had been a Boy Scout leader. I thought of the members of the congregation whose sons who had camped with him. I thought of the members of the church who had served on committees with him. We were traumatized. Evil had been with us. We had sat next to it. We had not come away clean. Knowing who the murderer had been was more fearful than not knowing. Now we knew the murderer was from us. He was among us. Many were still in shock. There had been a traitor in the congregation. We could not separate from it. It was there. The truth. How many would not return to church?

Mark Cabot: The Saiths' Cabin

We lived in Buckholt, a small town. We knew one another. But in knowing, we had not known. The authorities had come to the church. There was an investigation. I couldn't believe they were asking about Thomas Fout. A murderer in my congregation? One of my flock? Was not Judas chosen to betray? But what was the purpose of this?

Later that night, I could see the shapes of the furniture in the room in the cabin. The smear of dim light—it was a night-light in the hall in the cabin that served the same purpose as the moon I could see through the window, still spread across thin clouds. It was a lake house, I decided, more than a cabin.

I felt my depression returning. Even as a boy, I had heavy moods that weighed me down. I had taken medication. I had stopped the medication. My moods would plummet, then lift from time to time. I would handle them with my will. I felt the heaviness that pushed me into the bed. I thought of Scriptures written by others who had known despair. Out of the depths have I cried to you, O Lord. I wait for you more than they that watch for morning.[1]

That old asteroid, Satan, thrown from heaven, hit the earth with a thud. That old serpent, called the devil and Satan, who deceived the whole world, was cast out of heaven and fell to earth, and his angels were cast out with him.[2] Satan's purpose was to damage—to take what he could for his own. Wasn't that the point of Job? The enemy seemed to have access to dreams. To the depths of sleep.

I thought about Scripture again until the last, dim light of conscious thought turned off and I swam in the underlife on the other side of waking. A disk floated somewhere like the rings of Saturn. But the rings had moved to Pluto and they had squared. I saw the rings had atmosphere. There was a sky. The sky had wings in it. The wings had hooks. The hooks caught the clouds that floated past. Then I saw the rings were an open mouth. The mouth tried to tell me something, but I could not hear. The mouth enlarged. It formed the whole universe. Something terrible was there.

In the morning, I sat at the desk in the cabin and thought about my dream. Was Pluto still a planet? No, it had been removed from the list of planets. What was a planet when it was not a planet? A meteorite? No, a meteor flew through the sky. Pluto orbited with the planets. And wasn't

---

1. Ps 130.
2. Rev 12:9.

there the discovery of a new planet? Facts were always shifting, always changing, just as Clare got them memorized for school.

I sat with my head bowed. A disk was a circle in a square. My secretary had ordered some transparent discs. I had noticed the circle inside like the rings of a planet—not the disenfranchised planet that might not be what it was thought to be. What could I say to the bishop in his report? Thomas Fout was a member of my congregation who was not a member? Not a genuine member—that he only looked like one? Or was he a genuine member in whom something was terribly wrong? Was he a man like everyone else, but one who had found evil in himself and encouraged it, acted on it, thrived on it? Was evil in everyone? Was it like having a cabin one could choose to go to? Or stay away from?

I believed there was a force of evil in the world, and in the heart of man. The destroyer had arrived in my church. I was a minister—the minister of Christ Church—the shepherd of a small flock. Why hadn't I picked up on Thomas Fout? How could I have had a murderer in my congregation all these years, though Fout's murders were some years back, before I came to Christ Church? How could no one have known? How could it have been hidden so long? How would we get through this as a church? How had Grace and I gotten through our years of poverty? Our years of uncertainty. The loss of a child. The disappointment over an appointment at another church that didn't come.

I would get through this as I had gotten through it all: by faith. That's how I had managed. That's how I would continue. I was never sure of income because it depended on tithing, the giving of the congregation. I was never sure who was in my congregation—maybe a murderer—maybe someone was thinking of a criminal act while listening to my sermon. I could never be sure again. I felt violated, the way people felt when their houses were broken into. I'd been caught off guard. I had been a buffoon by not picking up clues. But what clues had there been? I was duped. I was angered. I wanted to abandon Thomas Fout. Deny he was a part of my congregation. He brought home the reminder of what we were capable of.

Lord, you know my downsitting and my uprising. You understand my thoughts. You compass my path. You are acquainted with my ways. Where could I flee from your presence? If I ascend to heaven, you are there. If I made my bed in hell, you are there. If I take the wings of the morning and dwell in the uttermost parts of the sea, even there your hand leads me. You possess my reins. My substance was not hid from you, when I was made

Mark Cabot: The Saiths' Cabin

in secret and curiously wrought in the lowest parts of the earth. Your eyes saw my substance, being imperfect. In your book, all my days are written.[3] Even this.

I knew also that Thomas Fout was fearfully made. But what had happened with this fearfully made man who turned murderer?

Did God know the terrible acts we would commit, but still chose to let us operate on self-will? Yes—we were free to act on our desires. Yes—God had to know. The terrible and even more terrible acts we have committed on earth were before him. Our history was full of horrors. That's why it took the death of Jesus Christ on the cross to atone for the sin within us.

Depression was a polder. I was below sea level. In my sleep at nights in the cabin, in my uncertainty of the way ahead, I felt broken. But hadn't the way behind been an indication of the way ahead? Had I ever been abandoned by God? Yes, when Tessa, our daughter, died.

Why couldn't I write my sermon? I woke in the morning a ghost of myself. My idea of what I could be was more than what I was. My wife, Grace, was grace to me—keeping the house, being my emissary, my ambassador. Our daughter, Clare, in seventh grade. Only one child to worry about, someone told me once. A daughter who had not caused us trouble as yet. Who would not. Who saw that the love of order opened up time for more important things. Who brought books and puzzles and video games to the cabin. Who could be by herself. Who was so quiet I sometimes wondered if she was there. How would this impact her? What would the children say to her at school? What could I say to ease her way through this? Could I even help myself?

What was this job I had—this ministry? Was it because I couldn't do anything else? Manual labor? Accountant? I had no father to go into business with like Roy Saith did. I had resented Roy's ease into his father's construction company. It was already there for Roy, while I had to plow the road. To go where it wasn't clear. To work with Biblical architecture that could not be seen. No, I had been chosen for the ministry, and in turn, I had chosen to do it. I was doing the Lord's work. I was in uncertainty, walking by faith instead of sight. I was in want. The rectory was in need of repair. The old car wouldn't always start. Our furniture was worn. I thought of the insecurity I felt when I thought of my bank account. Then the message: preach the gospel to every creature. Whoever believes and is baptized shall

---

3. Ps 139.

be saved, but they that do not believe shall be damned.[4] God often left no hard evidence of himself. Preaching would seem futile. It would be heartbreaking. It would be grace. He was. He is. He will be. There were times I would have done it differently than God. The I Am That I Am.

How could I explain the gospel more clearly? How could I explain it at all? I even had difficulty explaining it to myself. Was I supposed to follow God blindly on the road? Was I not allowed to question? Was I supposed to act like I was not disappointed?

I had wanted another ministry—had almost been chosen for it—a position in another church. But it had gone to someone else at the last moment. Was I supposed to believe I had been chosen to be here, in the middle of this? I got up from my chair. I sat down. I got up again. I walked down to the dock. I went back to the house. I paced.

Thomas Fout was president of the congregation. He was a compliance officer—an ordinance officer—in the community. Yet he had murdered and kept Buckholt under the siege of fear. I wanted to say, "*had been* the president of the congregation," but he still was, even as he sat in jail. There would have to be another election—soon.

Fout had murdered for years. Then the murders stopped. Had the murderer disappeared? Maybe he had moved away. Maybe he had died. Then, after many years, he resurfaced. When he was caught, I couldn't believe it was him. None of us could.

The investigators had traced him to the church. It was through the church that they had found him. Maybe he had given himself up. Maybe he knew what he had done in secret could not be hidden forever.[5]

What was the nature of man? What was the nature of his evil? Did everyone have it? Yes—according to the Bible, no one was righteous, no, not one.[6] Why did Thomas Fout not keep his unrighteousness in check, but let it out to prowl the neighborhoods? Why did he nurture it, develop it? Was it possible to understand the mind of a killer? The evil that was in all of us? It could not be denied. Fout was an ordinary man who went into the houses of others and killed them. He invaded their homes and took their lives. Why had evil gone so far in him? Did his wife not ask where he was when he came in late? Did she not smell death on him? How does murder smell? The intent to murder? The release when it was over? Did he come home,

---

4. Mark 16:15–16.
5. Luke 8:17.
6. Rom 3:10.

shower? Had his pupils stopped enlarging? Was he no longer swollen? Did Ruth Fout feel his heart still pounding next to her? Did he kill calmly? No, he had ejaculated. He had been aroused. Did he talk in his sleep? Did he toss? Was there knowledge of something she put away like a towel in a drawer? Did their dreams meet at night above them and kiss? His wife, with things in her house he had taken from his victims. She never found them? Or suspected? Had I? How could she not have known? How could I? Had Thomas thought of killing Ruth, his own wife? Did his children dream of it in their beds? Did the parents of any of the boys in Scouts suspect? Did Fout do anything that raised a suspicion we ignored? Some of his coworkers said he was arrogant, controlling. But most thought he was an ordinary man. No, it could not be. An ordinary man did not murder on his lunch hour and return to work. And how did he stop the murders after going so far? Did he step into an airtight compartment in himself, shut off from the part of himself that murdered? Did he just decide he could not do it anymore? How hard had it been to stop?

I was suddenly aware that the cabin was quiet. Grace and Clare were not there. Had they gone for a walk? Was I talking to myself? Had they overheard and left? Had Grace picked up on my wanderings?

God had made his will known in the Bible. He didn't impose himself on us. In fact, sometimes it seemed that he didn't care what we did. Yet he took notes. Our lives would be written before us when we stood at the judgment seat. The book would be opened. It was in words. Who was doing this writing? By writing we are known. We had been given freedom. Yet we were bound in a book: our will, our actions, our decisions. We had to account for our words. Even the idle ones. Would there be instant replay? Was there a leniency in this toughness? I didn't find it.

Heaven or hell was the choice. That was what the Bible said. I did not make it up. I was a minister. This was my territory. But the Bible could be bypassed. It could be ignored. It could be decided against as a conscious choice. The Bible could be left unread. But if it was picked up—if it was read and considered, if it was decided on as truth, a world opened. How could anyone argue with the evidence on the page? It was written by the Author. It was a book of murder.

17

Ralph Gheary
Confrontation

After Mark Cabot returned from Roy Saith's cabin at the lake, I approached him in his office. "You didn't call me yourself. You had Mildred call. Wasn't this something important enough that you should have called?"

"Yes, it was. I'm sorry."

"I thought you might have needed to share some ideas—some anguishes. I would like to have shared mine with you."

"I'm under duress. You can understand."

"Of course. I think Thomas Fout could be possessed," Ralph said.

"No. I don't believe that."

"How else can you explain how a Christian could commit these murders?"

"I don't know. How is your wife holding up?" Mark asked.

"About the same as I am."

"Which is—?"

"Barely."

"It's the same with us all."

18

Mark Cabot
The Sermon

On Sunday morning, I gave the sermon I had written at the Saiths' cabin:

"Why do I read those old parts of the Bible, unrelated as they seem? How can the Bible touch the place where I have found myself? Where the congregation has found itself? But there in 2 Kgs 13:20–21: 'And the bands of the Moabites invaded the land, and as they (the Israelites) were burying a man, they spied the band of Moabites, and cast the dead man into the sepulcher of Elisha, and when the man was let down, and touched the bones of Elisha, the man revived, and stood up on his feet.' Which was most distressing? The impending doom from the Moabites or the resurrection of this man they were trying to bury? It is a situation I know well. The Moabites are attacking. What have they ever done but attack in their many different forms? And here we are at a funeral, burying a man, and we have to get rid of him quickly because the Moabites are coming, and we lower the man into the first sepulcher we can find, which is the old prophet Elisha's, and the corpse of the man touches Elisha's bones, and suddenly the man we're trying to bury comes alive and wants to be lifted from the sepulcher. Does someone have another sword? What do we do with this death and destruction, this resurrection all at once—the absurdity of it all? I have let down my bones into the Bible and they have touched the holy words, those old prophets, and I am revived. What a reversal from what my life could have been.

One of Us

"Once again, the Moabites have attacked. I have nothing but Scripture to stand on. I have been dazed. I am beside myself. I am supposed to lead us through this confusion. The dust hasn't settled. At times, I feel half-crazed. I want to believe that what has happened is a mirage. Or I want to believe in the mirage that this didn't happen. People look at me in the stores. At gas stations. How vulnerable we are. How close to nothing. Even the sermon is a failure. The victims of Thomas Fout do not come back to life, on this earth, anyway.

"Yet I believe, if we live in faith, we will have strength to meet this situation. If we die in faith, we will see God. We have eternal life—even while we live. We possess it by faith. No matter how awful the circumstances though which we pass. We are washed in the blood of Christ. I believe that. I have to believe. I have no other way to deal with the horror. The Bible is relevant to my situation. The Bible is exactly where I find myself. It enters these terrible circumstances. It enters the destitution of the human spirit. It reaches us, no matter how far we fall. Through faith, there is a way out. This is what our faith is for—stacked against the day when all is torn down and we are found naked before God and others."

I heard women crying as I spoke. I heard men blowing their noses into kerchiefs. How long before a Sunday morning passed without sobs? Ralph got up from his chair in the sanctuary and went to Zelda, who sat on the front row beside her parents. He put his arm around her. She rested her head against his shoulder with her eyes closed. I was glad Grace could sit by herself. After the sermon, there was a weighted silence. I did not want a hymn.

"I know some of you have children in the nursery and Sunday school classes who are getting hungry. Anyone else who needs to leave—the service is adjourned. For those of you who wish, we'll remain in the sanctuary."

Probably half of the congregation left. Sunday morning was still riding the first wave of sensationalism, and the *dull* of religion had not returned—at least not until I asked them to stay for prayer. Other members of the congregation stayed in their pews: Roy and Beth Saith, Mildred Keller, the secretary, and her husband, Fred. George Weldon and Sam Stanton, whose wives left with a group of children, including the Saiths. Ben Ramos and his new wife. Ralph, Zelda, and Zelda's parents. Edna Fraiser and the others. I asked them to move forward. I got a chair and sat facing them. Our heads were bowed. There was a long silence. I prayed. I asked others to pray. I turned and knelt at the altar rail. Others joined me. We took turns praying.

Mark Cabot: The Sermon

Then our voices seemed to overlap as we all prayed with mumblings and cries we threw at heaven.

19

Zelda Gheary
The Drawing

Where were my art books? I looked through the boxes we had pushed aside when my parents came to stay with us. They had gone to the store, or on a walk, to give me time alone. I would stick my fingers into the books and rip the pages. I never had felt this violent. Who was this man to tear up our lives?

Art was larger than grief. Art was larger than rage. Art could do anything. Art was my defender. A help in the time of danger. But what was the danger? It was in the unanswerable questions Thomas Fout had left us with.

If anything upsetting happened, I could draw, and in the drawing, whatever happened would ease. I knew I couldn't be a painter, but I could still draw. Art would hold me. Even as what I knew fell apart, and in its falling threatened to take us with it, I would have art and my books, and in those places, I would be steady.

Why hadn't I brought the rest of my art books from my parents' house? There wasn't time to think when Mildred Keller called us about Thomas Fout. There wasn't time to think when Ralph pressured me to return to Buckholt.

I thought art could explain it all. If I could see it through art, if I could use art as a lens, a filter, a distorter of the distortion Thomas Fout delivered to us—I would be able to understand. But I was tired. Distraught. At the edge of myself. I was in hiding. I knew it to my own shame.

Zelda Gheary: The Drawing

Thomas Fout had opened the church to ridicule. The church with the murderer in it. I drew a black splotch in an old sketchbook I found in one of my boxes of art supplies. It was a door into a dark place. My drawings would be a helmet with a light attached to it. I would follow the light into darkness.

20

Mark Cabot
In Those Desperate Days

Sometimes my sermons were wings pinned to my arms. To pin on wings was to feel the suffering of others. To grow one's own wings was to know suffering itself. I felt the wing start to grow once again. Not the pinned-on kind, the kind that grew after a daughter's death. The kind that grew after the arrest of Thomas Fout. The kind that grew when I saw traffic pass the church and knew how insignificant Christianity was to them. If I could quiet my thoughts. which were running everywhere. If I would not be preoccupied. But that was what Christianity was for—to puzzle, to face the question of evil head-on.

    I wanted to follow Christ into the mystery and horror of a life that I was at a loss to explain. Christianity wasn't an easy out. I didn't want to be disturbed by peace. I wanted the turbulence of flight. I felt the pounding of my thoughts. I felt I was a fool. A dreamer. A hound. Hounded and hounding. How often did I pray and receive no answer? Yet there was no doubt. I believed God was there.

    Thomas Fout called again for me. The second or third time? The message was waiting when I returned from the cabin. I couldn't keep time straight. I couldn't keep events in order. They seemed to run into one another and repeat themselves in different combinations.

    The church had been smeared with Thomas Fout.

21

Zelda Gheary
Subworld

My parents didn't want to leave Buckholt, but I insisted. I knew they had to get back to Elwood. They knew it also, and they agreed to leave. A hundred times, my mother asked if I was all right. A hundred times, my father asked what was the matter. I was having trouble sleeping. I was upset over Thomas Fout. I was upset that Ralph and my new world had been shaken by murder. What was unusual about that?

When my parents were gone, I tried once again to paint, but realized it was not where I needed to go. It was not where I was capable of going. I knew it all over again. I sat in our bungalow with hardly any furniture. Eventually, Ralph and I would take a trailer to Elwood, to my grandmother's house. A church member, Roy Saith, had one we could borrow.

I opened the box of my drawings my grandmother had kept in her attic. I had thought to bring them back to Buckholt after the funeral. They were mainly drawings I had made as a child. They were crafted. They were kind. I felt I had been let out on the road. I knew I had to give up something I was not meant for. I cried by myself in the nearly empty house. Art would not let me down. It would remain my substance.

I could call people, get together with them, have lunch, but I knew I had to face this new self. I had to grapple with this new life, not run. I wanted Ralph to come home from the church and sit at the table with me. I could call and ask him. I think he would come, but I wouldn't bother him. I had to find my way. If I had to give up painting, I would not have to give up art. I got my sketchbook and sat at the table and worked—not painting, but drawing. I drew dark circles, smaller and smaller. There was some sort of *subworld* on my paper. A door into darkness.

I got out my art book and looked at Hieronymus Bosch's *Hell*. There were valleys of people in torment, driven by fear. People descending into a fiery pit. Some being sawn in half. Strung on the wires of a harp. Crushed by a mandolin. One was kissed by a huge groundhog. Nearby, a rabbit in a coat played a clarinet. Purposeless eternity. All for torment. As I drew, I heard some sort of singing in my thoughts: *They sang him a song from under the earth. They sang him a song from hell.*

What terrible force had seduced Thomas Fout? What tune had the demons played to get him to listen? Why didn't he recognize the musicians and know they were not from God? Why did he dance to the tune? He had to know. Maybe he thought he was Abraham with the directive to murder Isaac. But God provided a ram, and Isaac was not killed. Maybe Fout didn't find the ram caught in the thicket. Maybe he thought he was doing God's will. Was he that ill? No, he heard evil in his head and decided to follow it. Guided by demons that must have come around his bed at night. Who could lie beside him and not know? Maybe he kept it to himself so that even she did not know, maybe just as Sarah stayed inside the tent when Abraham took Isaac to the mountain.

As I continued to work on my *subworld*, I wrote the words that came from my imagination, making boxes or margins around the edge of the page in the sketchbook. *Did Sarah know what Abraham intended? Or didn't she? Did Ruth Fout know, or didn't she?*

I got up from the table and went for a walk. I felt weak and upset. I had to get out of the house.

22

Ralph Gheary
Holding Back the Flood

I had to defend the church for a day while Mark Cabot retreated to Roy Saith's cabin again. Zelda came to the church with me. Mark said he had to get away from the ringing phones to work on a report. I was tense as we drove to church. We still had to take calls from the members of the congregation and former members of the congregation. We had calls from the curious. Calls from news reporters. Calls from every small church in Kansas. Calls from Lutheran churches across the nation. We couldn't let the answering machine do it. It was clogged anyway. We took turns with the two phones in the church office. Usually Ben Ramos and Sam Stanton took turns at the front door. Mildred Keller, the secretary, had written what we were to say. The minister was not here at the moment. He would return. He had already said to the reporters what there was to say. We were in shock. We were trying to process Fout's arrest. I heard Zelda make a remark on her own, and I reminded her that it wasn't in the script of what we were to say.

23

Zelda Gheary
I Had to Have Something to Do

I drove to the college in Wichita to look for a job. I visited the art department. I had a BA and wanted to teach art, but there were no openings. I needed a master's degree. I found out I should be a student instead of an instructor. Where had I had showings? My college, when I graduated. Nothing since? No, it was just last year.

Where else could I look? Art had been eliminated from the public schools. Only the necessities were taught because of cuts. I could volunteer in a grade school in Buckholt. There were volunteers in the library who read stories to the children. Grace Cabot, the minister's wife, had done that. I could come certain days and be an adjunct, an art volunteer, an add-on. I could steal into classes and show them my art book. Not Hieronymus Bosch, no, he would stay in the bungalow with the new *subworld* drawings.

I stopped by a grade school one day and left my resume.

There were passages in the Bible I would call *painterly*. They were full of images. The Bible wasn't always clear. One had to *paint* their way through it. One had to imagine what was behind what was said. But that left it open to interpretation. Ralph was the interpreter. He wanted to explain. I was the questioner. I wanted to ask. I wanted to see in a visual manner. I was from a family in a small Kansas town without the funds to travel. Well, some did,

Zelda Gheary: I Had to Have Something to Do

but not my family. The fields of Kansas surrounding Elwood were a holy land to us. We lived and moved and had our being, so to speak. We felt it was much like the terrain of the Bible.

Jesus *drew* in the dust, we read in John 8:6. That was a verse I relied on—Jesus drew.

24

The Demons
The Gloat

It was one of the grooviest, happeningest things we'd done in a long time. Since we called farmwomen into the pond to drown, or Indians to raise their bows and arrows against settlers and return their hatred against them. We've played some marches. We've done some tunes. But a church member murderer is our pop tune. We made a strike. We made a hit. And tripped up the miserable little lives of these miscreants. Wipe them all out. Take them down. Put a thought in their head. Keep fanning until it flames. Help them stumble. Make them suffer. It isn't hard. How stupid they are. How loved by God.

25

Zelda Gheary
Another Hearing

Now there was another hearing, this one to charge Thomas Fout with murder. But Fout surprised everyone. He confessed to the murders. He told them in the way he wanted them told. He mentioned an x-factor that was the probable cause.

I hadn't wanted to come, but Ralph insisted. I sat beside him looking at the floor as I heard Fout list his victims by name and describe the method he used to kill them. I felt sick. I thought I would have to leave the courtroom. The ceiling was moving again. But Ralph sat with his hand firmly on my shoulder.

The next day, Ralph and I drove to Elwood to bring back some of my grandmother's furniture in Roy Saith's trailer. It was Ralph's turn to get away. My grandmother's house hadn't sold, but my mother wanted to clear her belongings out of the house. Ralph had hurried back to Buckholt after Fout's arrest, and we hadn't have time to look at anything. The house was crowded with people when we arrived. They were all asking, Do you want these? No, I don't—you can have them. No, I think she would want you to have them. What shall we do with this? What shall we do with that? Boxes and wrapping paper sat in the corners of every room. Piles were made to give to the church. The relatives shuffled through the drawers and closets.

Cars with trailers waited at the curb for larger pieces of furniture going to this cousin or that aunt.

I wanted my grandmother's cracked leather sofa with lion's feet. A metal typewriting table. Metal bookshelves. Anything sturdy, industrialized, utilitarian, functional. Ralph looked at the sideboard with a tin counter for rolling dough when I pointed to it.

"Are you sure you need all this?" he asked.

At least our bungalow in Buckholt would have more furniture in it.

We took my niece to the drive-in for a hamburger, then Ralph and I started back toward Buckholt. It was a slow trip with Roy Saith's trailer behind us.

26

Ralph Gheary
The Tin Man

We were silent as we drove back to Buckholt. The wind buffeted the trailer we pulled behind our car. Zelda looked through one of the art books she had brought from her grandmother's house. I thought about Thomas Fout as I drove. He became a tin man made of sheet metal and bolts. He became his own god and decided who lived and died. He was a wing nut. A nut and bolt with wings. He flew us to new places—fields none of us had known.

27

Zelda Gheary
History of Art

A neighbor helped Ralph carry the sofa and sideboard into our house. Two passing boys from our youth group stopped to help.

I saw Ralph limp as they worked. He had broken his leg as a boy. Sometimes it still bothered him. Ralph thanked the neighbor and the boys, and they left.

Ralph seemed impatient as we unpacked. He wanted to go to the church in case there was further development—in case something was in his mailbox.

"Stay with me," I said.

"I'll be back soon."

While Ralph was gone, I unpacked the art books and stacked them on my grandmother's bookshelves.

"Close the book," Ralph said when he saw the book I left open on the table to pick up whenever I sat in my chair to think, so I would know Christian art history. So I would know I wasn't alone. So I would know I had it easy. There it was. *The Martyrdom of Saint Bartholomew*, Giovanni Battista Pittoni, 1687–1767, skinned alive, starting under the arm.

"Put that book back on the shelf," Ralph told me.

Zelda Gheary: History of Art

"I leave it there so *I* can look at it. So I can know whatever we're going through has been gone through before, worse than we have it."

Ralph looked at me.

"*I* need them as a reminder," I insisted.

"But you're leaving them where *I* can see," he protested.

"What're we going to do?"

"About what?"

"About Buckholt."

"I'm looking. I'm watching for other openings. My advisor suggested it. I don't want the stigma. We'll have it—being here at the time of Fout's arrest. It'll be in my records that I was at Christ Church in Buckholt, Kansas, at this date. Anyone will be able to put it together."

"Where would you like to be?"

"With you, wherever it is."

"When did you talk to your advisor?" I asked.

"I talk to him a lot. We e-mail. Or talk on the phone."

"You haven't mentioned it."

"I'll tell you from now on."

"I'm your wife."

"I know."

"What you decide affects me."

"I won't do anything until I talk to you."

"I would like to know what you're thinking about doing before you do it."

"Of course," he said, "I won't *consider* anything until I talk to you."

But I knew Ralph continued to e-mail Harold Edwards about his worries. He was marked with Christ Church and the dilemma of Thomas Fout.

I had met Ralph in a history class in college. I remember even then he talked of the moral aspect of history. He was headed for seminary. I had always gone to church. I read Scripture. I decided I could believe because of the images I saw in the words and the religious paintings I studied. Jesus before the Sea of Galilee. Jesus talking to the multitudes.

We had said we would share every thought with each other. But there was a pulling away inside ourselves. I had my *subworld* drawings. There were things he wanted to consider without me. I saw how his decisions were not based on moral engagement with right and wrong, but on how these things would affect his ministry, his career.

One of Us

I sat with my eyes closed. I was not asleep, but thinking. How could I see the world the way I did? It was shaped by an irrational, irritating religion that I believed beyond belief.

I watched a program on the history channel as I waited for Ralph to return from another meeting at church, as if more meetings would resolve the dilemmas they faced. But they kept at it, those men, seeking to resolve what they had no answer for except the ever-present, runaway evil that broke loose from time to time. The world was full of wars and terrible cruelties, the narrator had said. The lessons of history. No, I thought, why blame history? The cruelties and tortures did not come from history, but from the people who made history. The difference between Hitler and Fout was that Hitler got the country to follow him. Fout worked alone. Hitler had others do his work. Fout committed his murders himself. It was a matter of degree, not essence.

I had the same viewpoint as Ralph—I mean, we looked at the world through a Christian lens. How it warped what was there. How it changed everything. How exciting to risk—to be ridiculous. What an adventure. I'd always loved the edge. I had lost friends who would not go as far as I would—this great distance into restraint, into resistance against a world without religion.

My name, Zelda, was short for Griselda, which meant, "stone heroine," or "gray-haired heroine," but I was not gray as yet, nor stone.

I was named after my lively grandmother, Griselda Foster, who died three days before Fout's arrest as though to escape what would happen. At least my mother shortened the name. Griselda was a character in Boccaccio, Petrarch, Chaucer's "Clerk's Tale," and had become associated with patience and wifely obedience. Yes, I needed patience. Why hadn't my mother named me the longer version?

I tried to explain Christianity. I tried to explain it to myself. It existed. It simply *was*. I paged through my large, gray art book, H. W. Janson's *The History of Art*. I looked at the Japanese print *Jigoku Soshi* (Hell Scroll) from the Early Kamakura Period, about AD 1200, paper, height: ten feet, National Museum, Tokyo. I read, "Christian last judgment with its anguished, naked souls and gruesome demons—although no western artist then knew how to depict flames so vividly."

The flames filled the painting like a bush or a huge, lovely, red flower with flaming petals reaching upward and enveloping the air. Two brutes ushered people into the flames with a club. I saw the open, wailing mouths of the people inside the flames.

Was it drawn after contact with missionaries? Or did cultures intuitively have a sense of ultimate reward and punishment that they worked to subvert?

Griselda. Grizzled—worried, fretful, complaining. Streaked with gray. Grisled was even worse, with its connotation of cartilage and gore. I remembered driving past El Dorado Lake with Ralph on the Kansas turnpike in a rainstorm. I remembered the wet, *griseous* air. Dead trees stood out of the lake—for fishermen, Ralph had said. Fog was rising off the water, which meant the water was warmer than the air. I remembered the drag of the car through the water on the highway. The rain hitting the windshield. The leafless branches of the dead trees standing in the lake reaching upward as if they were Jigoku Soshi's flames.

The next day, I worked again with my *subworld* drawings, pencil on drawing paper. I read the passage again about the rich man in Luke 16:23–24: "In Hades he lifted up his eyes . . . 'I am tormented in this flame.'" At noon, I turned on the news and saw the report of a man arrested for killing his girlfriend's one-year-old child. I put the sandwich down. I couldn't swallow another bite as I listened to the details of the beating: the broken bones, the fractured skull. The sandwich was a lump in my throat. I cried for the cruelty of men—and the cruelty of women. The mother who had done nothing to stop him.

I penciled in the flames for the torturers, the child-murderers. For everyone who had caused hurt to someone else, until the flames looked like waves on a lake of fire.

There was Alexander, the coppersmith from the New Testament, pierced by his own copper flames. There was Demas, forsaken as he had forsaken the Apostle Paul. There were the kings in the Old Testament, nearly every one of them evil.

Ralph and I held prayer each morning in the bungalow. He read the newspaper. He left for the church. I washed the breakfast dishes. I decided I could volunteer. I could continue to look for a job. I had to have something to do. I wasn't ready yet for children. I talked to my mother on the phone. I called Grace Cabot. I e-mailed friends. I wrote a note to my niece. It was still ten o'clock in the morning.

One of Us

I started a canvas, thinking once again I could paint, but I felt something dark in the corners and could not continue. I didn't know how to execute what I felt. I would leave it alone. I began drawing lines in my sketchbook. Where were they going? Our new marriage and pastorate had stalled. I drew boxes and filled them in with lead pencil. I thought of the Apostle Paul and the times he felt abandoned, betrayed, defeated by circumstances. He was preaching the gospel most everyone didn't want to hear. Yet he preached it anyway.

28

Ralph Gheary
So Much for the Poverty in the World

Appointed to Christ Church—Assistant Pastor, Youth Pastor, newly graduated from seminary. Where was the course on handling evil? Where was the course on facing a mass murderer in the congregation? What was this whiplash for the graduate hardly out of the chute? Where was the course on exorcism for a man who let the devil in, let him lead him like a dog on a leash, let him walk him where no one else wanted to go. How long did you look, Satan, before you found Buckholt?

I had been on the internet mapping the genocide in Darfur, Sudan. I had talked to the youth about missions and global awareness. I wanted them to know what was happening in the world. But murder here? In Buckholt? Zelda and I had talked about leading a mission trip. Before we were married, we had talked about becoming missionaries. It was Zelda who suggested it. I assumed it was her desire for travel. But I couldn't focus on that yet. I had been betrayed by a member of the church to which I had come. I had been betrayed by the seminary from which I had graduated. I had been betrayed by Mark Cabot, the senior minister who seemed to shut me out. I was included in all the meetings, but there was nothing personal between us.

I called my advisor, Dr. Edwards, for advice and prayer.

"I came like a lamb to Buckholt," I said.
"Then leave as a lion."

On Sunday night, I told the youth that questions and possibly even ridicule would come. We had to have answers for our faith. I broke the group into smaller groups of three. I handed out questions and visited the different groups as they discussed them. Zelda helped with the groups, though she kept swinging her crossed leg back and forth. I gave her a sign to uncross her legs and put both feet on the floor. We returned to the large group for more discussion.

I had a friend in seminary who had gone to Africa as a missionary. I wanted the church to support him. The missionary e-mailed photographs of a child eating a bowl of mush with a spoon as big as his mouth. There was another photograph of a girl carrying a child nearly big as she was. There were other photographs of people walking on a dusty path. The hopeless look on a child's face. The boy-soldiers. Rape. Murder. Injustice. Outrage. But how could I talk about Africa and our mission there when Thomas Fout was in the forefront? He had taken us from Africa. He had interfered with the message. How could we send missionary funds from a church acquainted with murder, a church now grim as an African orphanage?

I wanted to talk about poverty in Africa, but I was caught with a murderer in the driver's seat. Fout had murdered the opportunity to help. We were caught in the poverty of Fout's understanding. I had planned for my friend to visit Christ Church on his furlough. I wanted to develop our mission's outreach, but no one could hear anything except Thomas Fout.

I read the e-mails of my friend's field reports again. There was much I wanted to share with the youth group. Africa was the shape of a misshapen kidney bean. A twenty-five-hour flight away. A plane to Zambia. A bus to Solwazi. A dusty road to a bush village. Thatched huts made of termite dung and mud bricks. No plumbing or electricity. Boiled water with crumbs for supper. Death from AIDS. Tuberculosis. I imagined the trail of souls rising into the air. Heavy air traffic—the dead rising from the earth.

I wanted the church to offer hope, life. It wasn't a job for the African American community. They had enough to deal with on their own. I wanted Christ Church to send money to help plow a field, to build a church, a henhouse, a fishpond. Fout put a clamp on the church's desire to hear, to understand, to respond by giving. Our awareness of others was superseded

Ralph Gheary: So Much for the Poverty in the World

by Thomas Fout. What did a missionary mean to a church that had a murderer in its body?

Dr. Edwards called one afternoon and said a minister had died suddenly in a church in western Kansas. He asked me if I wanted to visit the church. I would also preach.

The next Sunday, after the visit to the church and a supper following the service, Zelda and I returned to Buckholt. I knew I would not take the pastorate that had opened.

29

Zelda Gheary
The Stunned Christ

I continued to draw a *subworld* on my paper, hiding it on the top shelf in the pantry of the bungalow when Ralph was there. I had never worked that way before. Sometimes I felt a strange heat as I worked, as if the oven had been left on—or as if I was nearing the inside of the earth. At first, the faces in my small drawings looked something like Edvard Munch's *The Scream*. I had to move away from Munch's man on the bridge. I had to find my own screams. I worked with mouths in small swirls. I drew ovals. Smaller and smaller.

Was there anything else other than Thomas Fout on the news, or in people's conversations wherever I went?

The elementary school never called about my offer. I would not have a job teaching art unless I went back to school. It was something to consider. I read the job offerings in the Buckholt newspaper with discouragement. What kind of job could I apply for that was not something I didn't want to do? How could I work at a job that was not a part of myself? Would I be satisfied anywhere? My thoughts were bouncing off walls I hadn't known were there. I was scared. I was shaking. I opened the Bible. John the Revelator spoke.

I saw the dead, small and great, stand before God, and the books were opened. And another book was opened, which is the Book of Life. And the dead were judged out of those things that were written in the books according to their works. And the sea gave up its dead that were in it, and death and Hades delivered up the dead that were in them, and they were judged, every man, according to their works. And death and Hades were cast into the lake of fire. This is the second death. And whosoever was not found written in the Book of Life was cast into the lake of fire.[1]

There—as if that settled anything.

My mother called about taking more of my grandmother's furniture. Her house had sold, and they continued to clear out the accumulation of her years. She wanted me to take bedroom furniture, but I didn't want it.

"We'll rent a bed when someone comes. This house is small. It's a bungalow. I work on my art in that room. I wouldn't have any place to work if it was filled with furniture," I explained all to my mother, as if it my art would make any difference. "You can store it for me if you don't want to get rid of it."

"What's the matter, Zelda?" she asked.

"I'm discouraged, of course."

"Come home for a while," she suggested, "Your father and I worry about you."

"I can't," I said, fighting back the tears in my voice.

My mother knew Ralph was not free to leave. I couldn't take our only car. My grandmother had had a car at one time. I had driven it to college until it would no longer run. Ralph and I could not afford another car. It was another reason I needed to work, not run back to my parents.

"I can stay with you a while."

"No," I answered, "I have to go through this myself. I can't leave Ralph. He wants me with him at the youth meetings. Everyone is struggling. Ralph and I visit some of the youth and their parents. We talk with them. We pray. I can't desert."

Back in my workroom, I penciled in hell. There was no escape. I continued to draw the ovals and circlings, but stopped. What if someone found my drawing? What if I had to explain myself? What if I was taken out and burned at the stake? It was incendiary. Hot as the inside of the earth. I couldn't face my life with art. It was too clear. Too revealing. It took me to a place I didn't want to go.

---

1. Rev 20:12–15.

I brought my book of religious art to Ralph when he came back, dazed from another day at the church.

"Look at this," I said. It was a woodcut, or pen and ink drawing. *Dead Christ with Angels*, Edouard Manet, 1866–1867. Christ was in the tomb immediately after the cross. The rock had been rolled across the opening of the cave. He was finally alone, still reeling from the trauma of the cross. He was staring into space, nearly in despair. Two angels were with him, equally despondent. One was crying, the other had its hand on his shoulder with a sorrowful look.

Ralph studied the drawing. The resurrection had not yet taken place. Christ was still in the aftermath of his suffering. But it looked like he had already come alive. Maybe he was thinking about descending into hell to bring back those he could. He had a moment to himself. The rock had not been rolled away and the tomb found empty.

30

Mark Cabot
There Would Be No Escape

I had a green chair in my study in the parsonage. Mornings I sat in it, feeling the nubs in the coarse fabric with my fingers. The chair was sturdy. Durable. I held to the arms of the chair with my hands. I rubbed my fingers over the nubs. It was comfort. It was real. It held me in the room.

I opened the Bible, anywhere, just opened it, put my finger on a verse, any verse: "who makes his angels spirits, his ministers a flaming fire."[1] That's what I was: a flaming fire. I was glad the Psalms were in the middle of the Bible. The pages opened easily to the middle. The Psalms were David's cries, his hopes, his anger. His words were a physical presence. I could read a verse of Scripture and it made an impact. I was not the smoldering pile of brush I felt myself to be, but a fire. Open the Bible anywhere. There was a step. A road. I got on my knees. I closed my eyes. I met with the living God. I leaned on him.

"Get me through this. Give me strength to—" my voice broke and I sobbed.

Thomas Fout had been arrested for murder. I went over it again for the board of deacons and the men's prayer group that met at the church. More than one murder—there were ten murders that were known.

1. Ps 104:4.

"Some men came to my office," I told the men. "They had evidence that someone from this church had sent a letter on a disk. They recovered erased files. 'Whose church duties were these?' I looked at the list. Thomas Fout. The president of the congregation. A member of the congregation for nearly thirty years. A Boy Scout leader. A murderer—a member of my congregation was a murderer. The investigators had to tell me several times before I understood what they said." My voice trembled as I talked. Roy Saith moved his chair next to me. What was wrong? "Tom has taken us with him into this. He's opened the church to scorn." I uncovered what was making my voice tremble—I recognized anger.

We prayed for what was ahead for the church. Ralph Gheary, the youth pastor and my assistant, seemed quiet. I noticed he limped. He said he'd broken his leg when he was young, and sometimes it was stiff. Others of us were visibly shaken, myself included. We trembled as a group. We prayed that we would have strength to answer the questioning. To face the humiliation, the horror, the responsibility I felt to the families of Fout's victims. Didn't everyone know something was wrong with churches—with those who went there?

It started again and again—taking us back to the beginning—the arrest of Thomas Fout. It was delivered over and over again. Faith was boot camp. It was militia. It was training for war.

What kept the wolf quiet year after year when Fout had torn flesh? How could I not have recognized the animal? The seed of evil that humanity had carried since the beginning. I knew a man's own will was going to do what it wanted. It was going to put God into a room and shut him away. It was going to say, "He is not here." It would say, "There are other gods." It would say, "The concept of the Biblical God is outmoded. People are responsible for their own redemption."

They would ask if redemption was necessary. They would say, "God is within us all. We just have to find him. When we find ourselves, we find God." What exactly did that mean? What would they do without the power of God to withstand the evil within? How would they withstand it, even with God? That was the line Fout had crossed—even with God, with church attendance, church work, he committed murder, annihilating the power of God. Not ultimately, but in his own case, Thomas Fout had negated God's grace in his life. But not in others. No, my congregation would endure. There would be resilience. That's what the Scriptures were—endurance I wouldn't have on my own. Why was evil within us? There was goodness

Mark Cabot: There Would Be No Escape

in each of us also. True. But ask the warring factions, "Where was brotherhood?" There was a murderous rage in man too. There was evil along with the goodness. I thought I had seen everything in my years of ministry. Terrorism in the world. Terror in our small community. Now there was this: terrorism in the church itself.

I faced more reporters who came to the church. I was slashed by the news. I faced the television cameras. I concentrated on remaining calm.

My wife had been with some of the women hiding Ruth Fout. They had gotten her out of the house after reporters began hounding her. They were at someone's house from the congregation. Grace wouldn't tell me over the phone. She was afraid someone would hear. I wondered if she was all right—Ruth Fout as well as my wife. Grace said Ruth was stunned with disbelief. It was the weight of a thirty-year-marriage to a murderer she couldn't shake off. What must his children, his family, be going through?

What power Thomas Fout must have felt when he sat in the congregation knowing he had done what no man had done—or probably what no man had done, at least not at Christ Church—and no one knew about it. How confident, arrogant. I could never be sure of anything again. That's what Thomas Fout had done to me. No, there were things I could be sure of—Christ was Lord. There were people who had visited the congregation. I felt the baggage that they brought. I couldn't name particulars, but it was there. It was something like seeing the flight of a hawk by its shadow across the edge of a field.

I felt the asymmetry of the life in Christ. As a minister, I had faced hard subjects. Eternal life in hell. Eternal life in Christ. Those were the choices, according to my understanding of the Bible. It was my job to tell them. I saw suffering. Anguish. Death. Now, murder in my own congregation. In the inner circle of my congregation. I thought how pain and horror was still with us, even in Christ. I did not want suffering. I did not like the thought that we suffered to build character, to know Christ, though it was true. I remembered Job: "I had heard about you with my ears; now I see you with my eyes."[2]

Evil. That rock that would not move.

I sat in the green chair in my study, rubbing my fingers over the texture of the fabric. The arms of the chair were a comfort to me.

2. Job 42:5.

Loss was another rock. Several years ago, our young daughter Tessa, who had contracted meningitis—mysteriously picked it up—slipped away from us. There was nothing we could do. Grace was unable to bear more children after Clare. We couldn't have gone through the possibility of loss again anyway. There was the talk of adoption. The decision against it.

"I think she is here sometimes," Clare said.

"Do you remember her?"

"I remember staying with others. I remember Aunt Ellie at the house—a lot of people."

Then there were the smaller losses, the ones that hardly counted in the face of the loss of a child. There were disappointments. Weariness, the feeling of being passed by, of not mattering. It was an invisibility I felt from time to time.

My other battles were mainly financial. How to provide for my small family on a small income? How to encourage church members in financial difficulty? How to pay church utilities? How to put gasoline in my car? How to pay for the next repair? The line of needy who came though the church for money or handouts. How to discern who was in genuine need and who was not. How to turn someone away when something did not ring true.

Grace, my wife, a minister's daughter, was at ease with it all. She could find bargains at the grocers. She could lead the family through difficulties and make it look like the difficulties were not there. She could visit the sick and help me in the pastorate. I felt at times that I could not do it without her. I could leave the house and return at night frayed, and she could put me back together. Yet she had shown little reaction to this. Was she all right after all?

Worse than the times that tore at me were the times when nothing happened. Another dull day at the church. A few calls. Another sermon to write. One couple in marital straits did not keep their appointment. Another couple did. What was there to do for them? How could they deal with their disappointment? God did not like divorce. God willed a union intact. But their hopes were rubble. How to settle for less? How to live without their earlier passion? How to know this was it for the rest of their lives? No, they had gone too far. The marriage was beyond repair in their opinion. But God could change hearts, I argued. He could change feelings. No, they didn't want reconciliation. They wanted to know the Christian way out. How to tell the children. How to attend church separately. At least the husband came to counseling. Usually it was the wife in tears because her husband was unfaithful. Often, the wife was willing to take the husband back if he would come to counseling. But that was not what the husband wanted, usually. He didn't want to come to the church. He would have to face his guilt in the house of God. If he stayed away, he could continue his self-deception.

But here was the point. I had had a man in church who had been in church not just for a few years, but for over two decades.

"You know," I told Grace, "I've had something on my mind several days. I kept thinking, What is it? I was embarrassed. Confused. I felt betrayed. A faithful member of my congregation was not only a murderer, but there was perversion too. He inflicted suffering before death with a slow suffocation. He didn't just break into a house and shoot people in their beds. The victims knew—their deaths were prolonged—they pleaded for their lives, I imagine—they were terrorized, panicked, in pain, horrified. It is anger I feel. Rage, actually. That's what was on my mind. I didn't want to recognize it. I was—*am*—utterly disgusted with him. How could he kill? How could he do that to them? How could he do it to us? The church. A Christian murderer. How am I going to explain that? How could he give me something like that to explain?" I knew it was murder I felt toward him.

I could almost hear the angry voices of the victims from heaven—get him—bring him down. Then God's voice quieting them—be patient just a little longer. Or maybe their voices were as mixed as the voices of the survivors. Some found forgiveness. Others wanted revenge.

Thomas Fout was a Christian. He was not a Christian. He was a Christian.

I sat in my office and wrote letters of apology and consolation to the families of the victims. I ignored a call from Thomas Fout. I told my secretary to tell him I was in a meeting. I ignored Ralph when I heard him talking to my secretary. I knew he wanted to sit and visit with me. I had thought about writing the letters ever since I saw the families in the courthouse at the announcement of Fout's arrest. I saw their suffering, their anger that remained after all these years. I saw my own wife growing paler all the time.

My office had been familiar to me. My wall of books arranged alphabetically. The file cabinets of my sermons, papers, and counseling notes. The arrangement of chairs. The photographs of Grace, Clare, and Tessa.

One of Us

My seminary diploma. My ordination papers. The spot on the rug where I spilled coffee. All of it as unfamiliar as if I sat in the office of a stranger.

31

Zelda Gheary
Where Do You Go When the Vultures Fly?

I continued with my *subworld* drawings. They were pencil sketchings of whirls and roads and pits and caverns. They were filling the bungalow. One evening, Ralph discovered them. Why was he looking on the top shelf in the pantry?

"What are these?"

"Drawings."

"Who made them?"

"Me, of course."

He stood there looking at them for a moment. "You're going to have to get a hold of yourself, Zelda," Ralph said to me, studying my *subworld* drawings he had uncovered, "You're going to have to let go of your art, if this is what it's going to be."

"Maybe it's how I'm handling all of this."

"There's something sinister about it," he continued.

"That's the point. I can put my finger on sin. I can understand what you're preaching against. I can know it by drawing it. I can understand the terrible condition of human life. I can feel our history. I can see the suffering in the world. I couldn't understand it without art."

"You don't need to draw hell to understand it."

"Maybe I do," I answered.

"It's getting you into trouble, Zelda," Ralph insisted, "What if someone saw them?"

"I want to draw. I have to have some sort of structure to hold onto."

"I thought we held onto the Lord," Ralph stated.

"Yes, but art is the instrument through which I function. We aren't all the same."

"I can see why you hid these."

"They're shocking," I agreed.

"They're horrific. How can a minister's wife get into this?"

"You have a murderer in your congregation and you asked how I got into *this*?"

"Have you always been morose?"

"Have you seen *morose* in me before this?"

"Do you want to leave Buckholt?"

"I'm just looking at the enemy—and coming to some sort of understanding with my drawings."

Ralph was upset with me. "Your drawings. Your attitude. Your sarcasm. You've got to hold back. You'll scare them. We're on rocky ground. We're still in the boat—"

"You're the last one I expected to turn on me."

"I haven't turned on you. I'm reminding you of propriety—of our office in the church."

"It's your office."

"It's yours as much as mine. Aren't you aware of your influence?"

"I don't think anyone pays attention to me."

"People's opinion of me depends on you too. You also influence me."

"Suppressing me won't work, Ralph," I said, "I have enough dousing by myself and my own work. I have a black wall here in front of me and nothing sticks but my *subworld* work. My flurries of anger and impatience. I would cover them with bones. Maybe that's what Fout found to do. Maybe that was his creative act."

"Murder?" Ralph raised his voice at me. "How could you say that? What haven't I realized about you?"

"That I'm a monster like Fout? That I could take the disappointment of our marriage and strangle it?"

I continued with my pencil drawings of the hell I imagined. I decided to focus on religious art that depicted Biblical scenes. I would study paintings. Art was still the world to me. It was more than words to me. Not the

Zelda Gheary: Where Do You Go When the Vultures Fly?

Word. But visual words that explained Biblical scenes, making them clear. I drew until my eyes felt dry. I continued to work. The hell I drew seemed to circle.

I understood Christianity in the circles of hell I drew. It was of everlasting importance to understand the gospel. It was not to be washed over. It was not to be dismissed. Christ had died on the cross for us. That was all that mattered. Otherwise people languished in hell. Therefore, I, a zealot, was established in my *subworld* drawings.

I worked on Dathan and Abiram falling into the earth as it opened its mouth in the eleventh chapter of Deuteronomy—their little chairs and bedding falling out of the tents as they fell—their little goats, legs sprawled—their camels with terrified eyes—their families with their mouths open in horror.

There was a women's Bible study and prayer group at Christ Church. There were always problems. A woman with too many children or a neglectful husband. A woman burdened with the care of elderly parents. Someone distraught. Overwrought. Disheartened. Sick. Hospitalized. It's what the church was for. A sanctuary. I made calls. I prayed. I supported Ralph. Our prayers seemed ineffectual since the arrest of Thomas Fout. Gaudy, actually. But how could prayer be gaudy? I mean, we prayed to the Lord, but it was as if Thomas Fout crawled around our feet. Our Bible study was a dip of our fingers in the dust—not knowing, really, what to *draw*. Both prayer and Bible study could be as sugary as Vacation Bible School. I was impatient. I worried about Grace Cabot. She seemed overly tired. I told her I would take the Bible lesson for women's prayer. I would shake them into the faith. I'd been reading too much Paul, Ralph said. Demas has forsaken me. Crescens has departed to Galatia. Titus to Dalmatia. Only Luke is with me. Alexander, the coppersmith, did me much evil. The Lord rewards him according to his works. No one stood with me, but all men forsook me.[1] Paul was in a city where no one cared. There were many adversaries.[2] Many who traveled with him left. It seemed that no one, or at least not many, listened. They all went their own way after his preaching. They turned their back on Christ. Yet Paul stood firm in his faith. This is the lesson I would have given if I didn't have to read from the stuffy guide to women's prayer meetings in the

1. 2 Tim 4:10–16.
2. 1 Cor 16:9.

church. I would set up a screen to show the history of Christianity in art. That's what I wanted to teach. I would share the images from my computer. I would show my *subworld* drawings. That's what it's like, this underpinning to life. Under-pine-ing. An underpine. A pine-ing under the earth. No wonder pines were in cemeteries. You think you're distraught now, just wait until the hereafter, when you see the living God and your place in the afterworld if you ignore Scripture.

I began giving titles to the *subworld* drawings: *Where Do You Go When the Vultures Fly? Where Do You Hide When the Ghouls Ride by*?

One of members of the youth group was in a play at the high school. Ralph and I went to see him. It was William Shakespeare's *The Tempest*. There was a line I heard: "in my false brother / Awakened an evil nature." Was that it? Yes, early in the play, that's what I heard. Ralph hadn't liked Shakespeare. He thought Shakespeare often sidestepped the truth of the gospel. But Shakespeare had read the Bible. There were references... Where were they? Ralph couldn't remember. He wasn't a Shakespeare scholar. He hadn't read the literature he needed to. He had enough books on Christianity to get through. Was Shakespeare like Emily Dickinson, who, it seemed to me, forsook the Christianity she heard? Or maybe just the way the church presented it. Christianity was a decision. Had she decided against it? Was that a fair question? Or had Emily just refused the outward form of it, one of the meaningless rituals of Christianity that seemed useless to her?

Thomas Fout was like the brother that Prospero told his daughter, Miranda, about—an evil nature had awakened in Antonio. He had given it opportunity. He had tended it. Watered it. And it grew.

Some of the people in church had children in a Christian school. I called and asked if I could volunteer for art days. I would go and talk about art history. I would give art lessons, though I know one of the mothers who had been in the prayer group opposed me. I didn't know it openly. I knew it from the reserve with which the others greeted me.

Zelda Gheary: Where Do You Go When the Vultures Fly?

I remembered the weight of the flannel graph drawings as a child. I wanted to make them significant for other children. I gave a few rudimentary lessons. This wasn't what I wanted to do. I felt confined. Thwarted. I couldn't get into the groove of the Christian school. I was having a hard enough time with the groove of Christianity. Why was what I remembered learning so different from what I tried to teach?

Here came a teacher with a sharp voice: "Do not pick up your brushes yet. Do not mix colors. Do not get your brush onto the table. Do not spill the cups of water. Do not make a mess."

I wanted to place my brush in her mouth. I wanted to color her invisible.

One day, the principal told me that some of the parents were bothered by the church from which I came. There was the taint of Thomas Fout. It would be better if I looked for work someplace else.

I always liked to read the names of colors on crayons. I often thought I would like a job naming crayons—cadet, asparagus, seaweed, hinge, rope, gallows, train track, kill kit. Maybe I would give them Biblical names. I wanted a conversion of color. I would like a job naming crayons: Whale. Babel. Zerubbabel. Revenge. Transgression.

32

Mark Cabot
Mephistopheles Himself

Thomas Fout called again, this time on my cell phone. I was in my office when it rang. He wanted to go over it again. The investigators had taken his confession. For two days he was with them. He understood law. He was part of them. Then they were gone and he was alone. I wanted to say, "Well done." But I was a minister. I had to find mercy. But it was not there. I had changed my cell phone number. Who had given it to him? Had Mildred talked to him? Or one of the lawyers? I wanted to drop the phone on the floor. Never pick it up again.

Was this more than I could bear? Was this someplace Christ couldn't reach? No, he knew where I was before I got there. I cut Thomas Fout off as he spoke. I had an appointment. The man was waiting outside my office. I closed the cell phone with a click.

I saw Fyodor Dostoevsky's *The Brothers Karamazov* on my bookshelf. I remembered the chapter, "The Grand Inquisitor": *Turn stones into bread. Jump from the cliff and not fall, but fly. Own the kingdoms of the world.* In those three temptations of Christ were the desires of men. I wanted to pick up the book, but a man had come to the church and a member of my congregation was now in my office. His habit had become a need. No, not drugs, but he had paved ruts he couldn't get out of. But God . . .

I invited the Holy Spirit into the conversation. I held a short interview. What exactly was the problem? I waited. I prayed. Had dialogue. Prayed again. I asked how he was feeling. It was hard to get my thoughts around

Mark Cabot: Mephistopheles Himself

the man's problem. I was preoccupied. I apologized as he left. He said he understood. I blessed him. Asked him to come back.

After Jesus' temptations, the angels ministered to him.[1] Maybe the angels would camp out here at Christ Church. I thought of Satan learning how to counterfeit, to pervert. Satan knew and used Scripture.[2] It is written, "their hands will bear you up."[3] But Jesus chose not to throw himself off the pinnacle. Thomas Fout had.

Ruth Fout called that afternoon. She was divorcing Thomas. She needed my help to expedite the proceedings. To testify about the necessity for the divorce. I agreed.

If I put murder in context, it wasn't that unusual. I reviewed it again in Scripture. I felt if I went over it enough, I would understand. In Biblical history, it was Cain, the firstborn of Adam and Eve, who murdered. But before him, God had killed an animal to clothe Adam and Eve. God wasn't for the fig leaves that they tried to cover themselves with. He had to do it by shedding blood.

The night that death passed through the streets of Egypt, the Hebrews put the blood of the lamb on the doorpost of the house— blood of the heart—and death passed over them.[4]

In the book of Ezekiel, there was a man, a scribe, who was instructed to mark the foreheads of those who mourned for the evil done in Israel.[5] They would be spared while others were slain in judgment. I was among those mourners of evil, but it had not come to me by choice.

I felt power as a minister, even the times I looked from the window and felt invisible. I felt God's presence when I spoke from the pulpit and when I spoke in prayer. Then this dart came through my flesh. I felt I had seen the face of Lucifer—I beheld Satan as lightning falling from heaven.[6]

1. Matt 4:11.
2. Matt 4:6.
3. Ps 91:11–12.
4. Exod 12:13.
5. Ezek 9:4.
6. Luke 10:18.

One of Us

There was that voice on my cell phone again. Thomas Fout, Mephistopheles himself, trying to resolve what could not be resolved. It had torn the church. It had torn me. I had seen the coldness in his eyes. I had felt the overwhelming urge to bolt as I sat in the visiting room at the jail across from him. Should I take my cross and hold it before him as we talked? How could I calm my rage? My raw nerves? How could I sit before him as the one in charge?

Grace called every morning and afternoon. We talked often, if only for a few minutes. Sometimes she stopped by the church. Why hadn't she called? Why hadn't she come by? I asked my secretary if she had left a message, but she had not. I wanted to tell her to call Ruth Fout.

I read the Bible for a footing. The fir trees rejoice with the cedars of Lebanon, saying, "No feller is come against us."[7] But I had been felled. I held the Bible in my hands and looked at it. The Christian had the New Testament overriding the Old Testament. Christ was there from the beginning. The Old Testament prophecy—he was brought as a lamb to the slaughter—[8]was fulfilled in the New Testament with Christ. The importance of the Jews for the Christian was that they carried the Christian heritage from the beginning to Christ, but they did not recognize him.

The Bible was the road I traveled, but where was this in it? What cave, what entanglement, what horror? How could I come out of it? What could I do? I was implicated. From time to time I sat in my office, unable to move. Other ministers called to ask how I was handling the Fout problem. The man had been in my congregation. He was still there, though he would not return. He would be imprisoned for the rest of his life. What lesson did he leave? What did the spot he left mean? Did he show us what a man was, in the depths of his heart? Why Christ died on the cross? Or was Fout someone whose wiring had been wrong? Not a threat to the rest of us. No, we could never do that. But Fout had punctured that thought or hope. What was the purpose of what the church was experiencing? God allowed murder and sorrow and rage and pain. He had placed a mark upon Cain. Now the congregation and I bore the mark.

I thought of the faces before me on Sunday morning, longing for me to turn this stone to bread. They were faces I knew well. Jack Kester owned

---

7. Isa 14:8.
8. Isa 53:7.

Mark Cabot: Mephistopheles Himself

a small plumbing company and had fixed the leaky faucets at the rectory. Next to the Kesters were the Saiths. Roy fixed the church roof where a leak had rotted out some timbers. These men gave of themselves. I looked over the congregation as I spoke that morning. I saw the weary. The stunned. The confused. The nominal. The barely there. The zealous. The committed. All of them sat before me on Sunday mornings.

Yes, Fout was one of us. One of us, as Cain had been.

I cut short several calls in my office. I grew impatient with anyone not a murderer. I didn't have patience with anyone's sick aunt. I had no desire to make hospital calls.

Was Thomas Fout pushed down until he broke loose? He killed, and the pressure was eased for a while. But how did he make it at the end? How did he not bolt? How did he stop killing all those years? How did he hide it? But had he? He had told a reporter that he planned to kill again. He knew who his next victim would be. The killing urge was on its way back.

Fout must have popped up on God's radar long ago. When he was born, God knew him—before he was born. Yet God gave him choice, giving him room to decide against murder, but he would not.

How had he sat in the congregation all these years, heard sermons, gone home with his family? How had he seemed so normal? How could he have brought us to this? He wasn't thinking of anyone but himself. It was all about him.

I felt a brittleness at our supper table that evening. Often we had others at the parsonage for supper after church, but Grace had not wanted anyone to come. She forced a conversation about something. Clare talked about an event at school. She had begun to have nightmares. Strings were floating toward her. They bound her. Tortured her. Killed her. For a few nights, Clare slept between Grace and me.

Once in a while, Grace slept with Clare.

33

Zelda Gheary
A Prayer for Ruth Fout

Mark and Grace took Ruth Fout to the divorce hearing. I went with them. I would go with her afterwards because the Cabot's had someplace else they had to go. Others in Ruth's family had to work. Her grown children had returned to their homes in other cities. I, of course, was the only one with nothing to do. The divorce had to be immediate. It was an emergency. Ruth Fout couldn't wait the required time. There were extenuating circumstances in the case. The judge decreed the divorce. She left the building sobbing. The Cabot's helped her down the stairs. Where had the evil come from that left us with a shell of ourselves? What god allowed that?

I broke a dish against the sink by accident that evening as I was thinking of Fout and the grief of his wife, now his former wife. I was washing dishes, though they fought against me.

I called Ruth the next day.

"They see me come and go," she said, "I cover my face. They go to the marriage records. Find our names. Go back to my high school picture. They wait outside the house if I go back for anything. I'm stalked. Threatened. Spit on. Run from."

I wrote a prayer for Ruth Fout around the edges of my *subworld* drawings:

Zelda Gheary: A Prayer for Ruth Fout

The Lord is my shepherd I do not want. He leads me into black pastures. I walk beside the putrid waters. I am not restored. I follow the path of unrighteousness. I walk through the valley of the death of shadows. There is nothing to stop the knowledge that burns into my brain. I fear evil. I have slept with it for years. A rod discomforts me. I am ripped. I am torn apart. My table is set in the presence of enemies. My head is anointed with scalding oil. My cup runs over. Surely this evil will follow me all the days of my life. I will remember it in the house of the Lord forever.

34

Mark Cabot
Rhododendrons

The men's prayer breakfast was a small group. Not everyone could bring themselves to attend. Sometimes news reporters were still outside the church, hoping to talk to someone with another piece of information about Thomas Fout. Every time there was a murder on the evening news, it would come back. It was hard to face. There was a silence in the room. A suppressed anger. An awkwardness. Thomas Fout sent us slogging once again to Bethlehem.

"His eyes are on the ways of man," I read, "There is no darkness where the workers of iniquity hide."[1]

The other men read from different passages of Scripture:

"My eyes are on their ways, they are not hidden from my face, neither is their iniquity hidden from my eyes."[2] Albert Furnish, who was the father of Catherine Ramos, Ben's dead first wife, read a similar passage.

Roy Saith read about the plummet in the hand of Zerubbabel.[3] Yes, the plumb line would be Roy's offering. As a builder, he knew what a plumb line meant.

We tried to reach an understanding of Thomas Fout, who had acted as though he had the power of life and death.

1. Job 34:21–22.
2. Jer 16:17.
3. Zech 4:10.

Mark Cabot: Rhododendrons

"The eyes of the Lord run back and forth throughout the whole earth, to show himself strong in the behalf of them whose heart is perfect toward him,"[4] I read. "We all know we're far from perfect, but we're covered by the blood of the perfect one. When God looks down upon us, he sees the blood of Christ and we are counted righteous. That is my hope for Thomas Fout." I ended the meeting.

The men stood. I could tell by the discomfort in the room that we all were struggling with the thought of God's forgiveness for Tom.

What could I say to the congregation that would matter? I saw their faces lined up again in rows on Sunday morning. Many of them sat in the same pews week after week. How could I answer the questions? What would persuade them there was hope that we would ever be the same again?

Jack Kester would stay after church to make a repair in one of the bathrooms. Other men would stay for prayer. Their wives and children would go on home, or stay talking together in Fellowship Hall while their husbands prayed or worked. Was that my job anyway? Wasn't I just supposed to deliver the message and then leave it to God? If they were blind to my message, they were blind to God himself. If they rejected me, it was God they rejected. What could I say of God's strangeness? His unwillingness to explain himself. How could I ease my people over the hard parts? If I could not give the guidance they needed, church was just like anyplace else. The last place people would want to come for answers. And Jesus—hadn't he been rejected long ago? Leave him in the dust of Galilee.

On Tuesday, I had a meeting at another church. It was an ecumenical meeting. Pastors from different faiths in Buckholt got together from time to time. We prayed for the town. We prayed for our congregations. We talked about how to build membership. How to stop the erosion of members. We prayed for Christ Church. We prayed for each other. I was the recipient of most of the prayers.

The speaker that afternoon talked about Islam. Islam in Kansas? Yes, it was on the rise. My first thought was that I wanted to be with Christ, not Allah. I heard the call to understand other religions. What was Islam?

---

4. 2 Chron 16:9.

A set of rules. A government or state. Who was Allah? An idea of men? They ignored the message of Christ and shaped a god with their own hands. They would get to paradise by their own efforts. Impose their own ideas on God—their ascetic inventions. Did Yahweh work along the lines of free will? Did he stand back, then later destroy those who didn't come to him by their own will—their own faith in the blood of Jesus Christ? He that acknowledges the Son has the Father.[5]

We had another meeting at the church to accommodate the shock waves that rolled over us. The meeting began with prayer. A request for wisdom. What would we do? We had sat next to a murderer on Sunday mornings and in our meetings. Our sons had been in his Scout troop. We had been alone with him in the church. We kept going over and over it. We were stuck in a muddy field. Our wheels were spinning. We felt we might never find our way out.

What are we going to do? The questions repeated themselves. Christianity had taken another hit. What kind of religion was it? Hypocrites. Harboring criminals. There were strange people in churches. Often the desperate with nowhere else to go. Church attendance was something to substantiate them.

"He came to church and acted like one of our own."

"Look what he's done to us."

"Then you can be the one to cast the first stone."

Rhododendrons. Those flowers in my mother's garden. What were they doing in my thoughts? How stress inserted odd thoughts. Yes, I would remember flowers. It wouldn't be work in the garage or basement or field. It wouldn't be a man's labor. I had felt left out of all that. I had a different way to go. I would labor in the gospel. I would see more flowers than I wanted at funerals and cemeteries and church altars and even marriages that I knew probably would not last. Yet I had to speak the words of holy matrimony before them, knowing they would walk on them as if on gravel.

---

5. 1 John 2:23.

35

Zelda Gheary
The Ceiling

> It is so peaceful on the ceiling!
> —Elizabeth Bishop, "Sleeping on the Ceiling"

I had found an old stepladder in the back of the garage when I painted the second bedroom. I carried it into the house and into the room where I worked my *subworld*. I set it in a corner. I climbed the ladder to a corner of the ceiling. I drew a small circle. I felt creepy. I felt spooked. I felt danger.

I planned to paint this room also. I could mark on the walls and ceiling before I did. I drew another tight little circle in the corner of the ceiling. This was the job I had found—tossing my ball of anger. No, I had balls of anger. I wanted to rid myself of them. I shuddered in horror. I drew another circle in the corner of the ceiling.

36

Mark Cabot
The Ministry

I longed to be with my wife as I sat in my office. Why had she become distant? I felt more than myself when I was with her. She was someone I belonged with. Someone I felt whole with. Someone I had to protect. I wanted to tell her not to answer the phone, but it might be someone who needed help. If it was a reporter, just tell them to contact the church. The church phone had been busy. My secretary was sheltering me as much as she could—shedding, shuffling, warding off the incoming.

What could I say? How many reruns in my own mind could I endure? The bishop had been beside me when the reporters hit. When the floods came. Yes, Thomas Fout was a member of the church. Yes, they tracked him here. The church was a place for killers. Jesus died on the cross for the lost. The untoward. The warped. The framed. But Fout was not framed. He was guilty. He asked to see me when they took him to jail. He told me that he was the murderer. He had confessed. He apologized. He was caught. Maybe it was a relief, though he didn't say it. How hard was it to hide himself from God? No, there was no hiding from God. He could get away from it for a while. Circumvent it. Slough it off. "Slough." That was the word. If only people flocked to my sermons like news reporters to the church.

What questions would they continue to ask? The local news as well as national, and the documentaries I knew would come. What would they say? My church was caught with its pants down? How would I explain it? How could I understand it myself? This man who was part of my congregation.

Mark Cabot: The Ministry

He took duties upon himself and executed them. This man had been reliable, faithful, dependable. He attended church regularly. How had his pastor been duped? That's what Fout had done. Duped me. Was he a man struggling with his past? Was he a man struggling not to murder again? Was it a genuine struggle? Was he just trying to cover his tracks? Was he repentant all these years? Had he wished he had not done what he had done? Yes, we had been caught with a wolf in our pasture. A murderer in our midst. The Boy Scout leader, the murderer. The family was devastated. Fout's brother had to return to Iraq. The mother was old. She didn't want to understand. Maybe she hadn't even been told. Fout's wife, Ruth, was still in shock. She wouldn't return to their house. The news vans were there with their antennae like huge beetles. Their cameras glaring. Their intrusive invasiveness. Our decimation was their life-blood.

What would we do? Be made fun of, certainly. Mocked. Yes, the Lord had been mocked. His beard had been pulled. His forehead stuck with thorns. How would he hold up his head? Open the Bible. Find a verse from the Psalms. Lay ground with Scripture. Stand on it. I would face the probe with dignity if I could. The questions. The doubt this would put on Christianity.

Later, at home, I sat with Grace and Clare at the dinner table. I prayed again for strength for us, for the Fout family, for the church, for the families of the victims, and for the helplessness, terror, and pain they knew their relatives faced before their deaths.

I talked to one of the victim's children, who could think of nothing else. He turned from me. How could he worship with rage in his heart? Revenge was in all their hearts. They could murder in return. It was natural. Logical. The seat of evil was in the human heart. It was a spiritual force in the world. The bad and good angels. Was it that simple? Did they float about in heaven, spearing one another, storming one another's fortresses as they did in the Middle Ages with their catapults and fiery arrows? I reminded myself once again that it was the reason for the death of Christ on the cross. When would these after-shocks pass?

Did spiritual forces send their powers on earth to see what kingdom they could rule? To see what dictator they could persuade to torture their people? To hold their reign by force? To see what could be done in the name of Satan, making a mockery of his name? Satan made me do it. Did it make a horrifying truth laughable? Dupe them into laughing at Satan. He didn't exist. Let them not name evil. Let them circumvent the concept. Let them think it didn't exist, or only existed in monsters such as Hitler and the hit list of mass murderers. Let them think they could face the ultimate reality on their own. Let them say there is no ultimate reality. Let them think there is no heaven or hell. Let them say they created their own hereafter. Or there was no hereafter at all. That when they died, they were dead. The truth of the matter was that when life was created, it lasted forever. They were here to decide where they wanted to spend life after death. But what to do with Fout? What to do with the idea of Fout?

I thought of the awkward Sunday mornings when we gathered for church. The new faces—some of the old ones gone. What to say? How to say? How to sit calmly before the congregation as we sang hymns? Then open my mouth in prayer. Continue with my sermon. How to speak to them of the unfathomable?

I had never ridden in a rodeo. I had rarely been to rodeos. But that is where I felt I was.

Two of the men in my congregation called and took me to lunch. We talked about baseball. We talked about fishing. We talked about anything but Thomas Fout.

When they drove me back to church, I was afraid I would choke up as we said goodbye—because of the understanding they showed me, and because of their act of ministry to me.

I opened the Bible again to Ps 104. It was about the floodwaters. A torrent of rain had fallen on the church. Thomas Fout was the reason. It continued to fall. The rain was needed, especially in the drought of late Kansas summers. But now it *over-rained*. The water could come so far and no farther. But I felt it cover me as I sat in the green chair in my study in the parsonage. I got in my submarine, which was what the Scriptures were to me. It was the only dry place at the moment. The only place the floodwaters could not come. I was the pastor of a small church in a small town. I could not find the sky. I rode in my submarine. I would speak the waters back. I would rise to the light of his word.

37

Ralph Gheary
A Visit with Thomas Fout

I went to jail to see Thomas Fout. I wanted to find out what I could about Fout without Mark Cabot between us. I had thought about demon possession. I read Scriptures on demons. I decided that I believed in them. How else could someone murder people they didn't know? They had not been murders of passion without forethought, when a man suddenly discovered himself betrayed and lashed out at the betrayer, or found himself on drugs and tried to steal with someone standing in the way. These murders had been calculated. They seemed like the work of demons.

I felt anxiety as I entered the jail and sat across from Thomas Fout in the small room. Would Thomas threaten me? Try to murder me? Would Thomas confess his sins to me?

I found Thomas Fout unrepentant, dismissive, distant, arrogant. Fout only wanted to talk to Mark Cabot. He only wanted things his way. I was disappointed as much as relieved. This was not a demon. This was a man in his right mind, but his right mind was not the right mind I considered right.

"I was willing to give you the benefit of the doubt. I was willing to believe you were possessed, " I told him, "I hoped that responsibility was somewhere else. But I see you before me now. I remember when you stood at the hearing and confessed to the murders. You were cold, calculated. You had run a business—murder. You had killed methodically. It was thought out. I've changed my mind about possession. It wasn't the x-factor you've mentioned to excuse yourself. It was forethought and intent to murder."

Fout looked away, ready for me to leave. It angered me.

"Zelda, my wife, was never fond of you. I remember once she said she couldn't sit in the same pew and moved back from you. You didn't know it. You were thinking of your next murder." Thomas Fout stood, but I kept talking, "I'm beginning my career. I've been marked by Christ Church. It will follow me all the days of my life. But I will dwell in the house of the Lord forever. I'm not sure you will."

"You should examine yourself," Thomas said to me.

"I just graduated seminary. I thought I had God figured out. I could contain any problem that came to me. But here comes Thomas Fout, who murders all I thought I knew. You've shaken everything I know. Why didn't God strike you with lightning that Sunday people were running to their cars in the storm? I thought lightning would crack open the sky. Mark Cabot can hold his opinions, but believe me, he thinks as I do. Your former wife turned her back on you, changed her name. She'll get rid of your house, and you have nothing to say about it."

I realized I had turned into a madman as I vented before Fout. I had the power to stop myself, but I chose to continue.

"You're evil, in my opinion. I don't care what you did, but you did it in the church. You brought your evil inside the church I have vowed to serve all my life. What do we do with the smudge? With your attempt to restructure faith—to tear down—to distort beyond recognition—the thought that you can murder these people and wreck the lives of the families they left behind, yet you'll sit in heaven?"

"I got to you, didn't I?" Thomas turned and walked away from me.

"Your sentencing is coming up. You'll sit in prison and know the world goes by without you. You've been removed."

I walked from the jail still enraged. Was there no end to my anger? I hadn't even gotten to the consequence of Fout's sin on our missions. I hadn't told Fout how he interrupted my work in the mission field—how I had to tell my friend I would have to get back with him about the commitment of Christ Church. It was preoccupied at the moment with one of its members.

Had I committed a sin? I asked myself that question again and again as I crossed the parking lot and drove through the gate. Yes, I had. I knew what I was doing, but I went ahead with my venom, just as Fout must have done as he stood over his victims. In the same way, I sliced it into Thomas

Ralph Gheary: A Visit with Thomas Fout

Fout, who had caused me pain. In doing so, I found out more about myself than Thomas Fout.

38

Zelda Gheary
Upper Room

I placed my drawing paper on my grandmother's sideboard, which I kept in the semi-dining room that was part of the bungalow's living room. I ran my drawing pencil over the paper, over it and over it, picking up the notches, cracks, and dents my grandmother had made in the tin counter over the years. Then I erased small whorls on the paper. The Apostle Paul had murdered also. He admitted it in Acts 22:4, as he stood giving his assent to the stoning of Stephen. He persecuted to the death when he was Saul. The whorls on the paper were the open mouths of the believers he persecuted when they heard he was now preaching the gospel. They were in the afterlife, but they had received the news. *Vugs.* Isn't that what they're called? Little cavities of mouths opened in disbelief. But the believers would not be in the *subworld*. I had to focus on unity in my work. I had to return to the *subworld*. I titled my work that morning, *"Their children dashed to pieces, houses spoiled, their wives ravished"* (*Isa 13:16*), which I wrote in a lower corner of the drawing.

Maybe Thomas Fout was in prison preaching to the convicts. I mean, maybe that was God's will for him being there. I felt unraveled at that thought. I felt something crawling through me. I felt something clash. How could this world be understood?

In the upper corner of my drawing I wrote, "Deut 14:13–18: Thou shall not eat the glede, kite, vulture, pelican, sea gull, swan, owl, lapwing, bat," and left my work for the day.

39

Grace Cabot
The Pastor's Wife

I had to call Ruth Fout. Who else would bring her to church? It was not something we could ask anyone else to do. But Ruth would not go.

That evening, Mark and I drove to the relative's house where she was staying. We took a circuitous route in case a reporter had been assigned to us, but we saw no one following. Ruth cried when she saw us, wringing her arms, trying to get her marriage off her. Mark and I prayed for Ruth as she sobbed. Mark spoke to the relatives that remained in the room with us. We were all in tears over the shock. The shame.

Afterwards, I asked Ruth again about church.

"I'm not going."

Mark assured her I would sit with her.

"He murdered—" Ruth said, "He murdered our marriage. He murdered part of me."

"He murdered a part of all of us," I told her, "but we get up and go on with what we have left."

40

Zelda Gheary
Zelda Leads Women's Prayer

Grace Cabot asked me to give a talk at the women's prayer meeting at church. I looked up "woman" in the dictionary. "Wolves." "Woman." "Wombat." That was the order.

I had religious paintings to show them. Christ and his mother. Christ and his angels. Christ and his flock. Then I presented the thought of abstract Christian art. It began in Genesis. God spoke the world into being. Imagine a tree coming from the mouth of God. Imagine. I talked for half an hour, then Grace Cabot rose from her chair.

"Thank you, Zelda," she said.

I had more paintings to show. More work to talk about. But I sat down as the women clapped politely.

The large upper circle of my *subworld* drawings was for those who were locked in the self where they had chosen to be. They had chosen to do wrong. They hurt others—the main one being Christ by the rejection of his salvation. Always back to that cornerstone of the Christian faith. What did they do in hell? They anguished, grieved, raged, and regretted. Whatever they were in their thoughts on earth, they carried with them after death, shouting out but not communicating with one another. There was rampant darkness in the heat. They'd been turned inside out. They would be that way forever. I wrote words I read in the Bible that morning: "When lust has conceived, it brings forth sin, and sin, when it is finished, brings forth the death."[1] That separation from God. And once in a while, from the upper realm, a breeze that was an unbearable song from heaven. What did they think that Scripture meant? Words continued to be a part of my *subworld*.

---

1. Jas 1:15.

41

Mark Cabot
A Snake at the Saiths' Cabin

I think Roy's family had planned on going to their cabin Friday and Saturday, but they knew I was in need of it. There was a word I found, "piscary," which meant the right to fish in another's waters. That's what I was claiming at Roy's cabin, though it was a right I defined for myself with Roy's permission.

I watched Clare pack her books, paper, pencils, workbooks, computer games, a doll that hardly came out of the suitcase anymore. She looked forward to playing with the girl down the road. I realized how important it was to have someplace to go, to get away, to have a destination to look forward to after a week at school or work. I tried to forgive families who didn't come to church for weeks because they had a cabin on a lake.

What a man Roy Saith was, I thought as I looked at the cabin. A builder, a contractor, with spiritual and intellectual interests. Roy thought about things—he was fair-handed. He should have been president of the congregation, but he was too busy with his work and family. I looked at the books on a small shelf in the room I used as a study at the cabin. There were books on architecture and a few novels. What would it be like to own the cabin? What would it be like to have a father who pulled me into his line of work? The sort of work at which Roy excelled, yet there was a hunger for God in him also.

Mark Cabot: A Snake at the Saiths' Cabin

I opened my mouth and panted, for I long for your commandments. Look upon me, and be merciful.[1]

I was walking to the dock in the morning with Clare and the girl from down the road, when I saw the snake. I called the girls away from the dock, suggesting they walk down the road. I returned to the dock a second time. Grace had gone to the store. There it was, beside the concrete ramp into the water. A snake with brown markings on its back. It was dull, almost like the leaves, but its nose looked wet. It was sluggish, not moving. Was it dead? Had it just come from hibernation? It hadn't been there before. Had something left it there? The snake was moving now, slithering slowly back toward the ramp. If it got under the ramp, I would not be able to get it. I would not be able to let Clare play by the dock. I would know the snake was there. I had no instrument. I called to a man next door.

"Have you got an ax?"

"No."

"A shovel?"

"Yes." The man went to the shed to get his shovel. The snake continued toward the boat ramp, disappearing partially under the ramp, its head now out of sight. Soon the whole body would be gone. I looked for the man, who was not yet on his way.

"I command you to stay still," I said. "I have power over you by the blood of Christ. Your head is wounded.[2] Jesus took power over you."

I stood as still as the snake. I knew then the man was returning. He handed me the shovel. I lifted it in the air and brought it down on the snake's back. It writhed. I was sure I heard a cry—a tiny cry. Did snakes cry out for their lives? The leaves cushioned the snake. The shovel could not break the bones. I didn't have the strength because I was at an odd angle that didn't give me leverage.

"Do you have a knife?"

"No."

"Anything?"

The man thought, but he did not. He seemed unable to do anything.

I continued to hold the shovel on the snake.

"I have another shovel."

"Good."

The man left again for another shovel.

1. Ps 119:131–32.
2. Gen 3:15.

The snake's neck and head were out from under the dock. I twisted the shovel, trying to cut into the snake. The snake opened its mouth, lunged at the shovel again and again, striking it. A water moccasin? A harmless brown snake?

The man returned with the second shovel. With one hand I held the shovel holding down the snake, while with the other hand I lifted the second shovel and rammed it into the snake's neck. It writhed again.

I still couldn't kill it.

A trawler passed in the cove. No, they didn't have a knife.

The neighbor had a son who worked for the fire department. He called him.

They came in their red diesel truck. I heard it on the road before I saw it.

They carried an ax. They looked at the snake. It was bleeding by then as it struggled to get out from underneath the shovel. One of the firemen jumped on the shovel, breaking the snake in two. Its head jumped free and flew toward the firemen's legs. They all jumped back. It still wiggled on the ground—both parts of it. They stood looking until is movements were indiscernible. Finally they threw the two parts into the lake.

The girls came then. They had seen the truck. And Grace was back from the store with groceries.

"What's going on?"

What could I say? "I found a snake."

"A snake—here?"

"This is a lake, Grace. It was harmless, but I killed it in case it was poisonous."

"You couldn't tell?" Grace was taking groceries from a sack. She dropped a box, and out of frustration, kicked it suddenly with her foot. Clare and her friend stared at her. Grace started to cry. She hit the sack. I grabbed it away from her and told the girls to go outside.

"Your mother is upset. Leave us alone for a while."

Grace kept pounding. Now it was the counter where the sack had been.

"I don't like to come here."

"It's all right, Grace. We're going back tonight. I'm in the middle of a sermon—I can finish before dark."

"I don't like this place—this world full of evil."

"Why didn't you tell me you don't like to come to the lake?"

Mark Cabot: A Snake at the Saiths' Cabin

"Why didn't you know?"

I pulled her to the table where we sat until she was calm.

Evil. What was it? A strain in the world? Dictatorships? Cruelties of government? Look at the world's history. Look at the evening news. Look at unruly children in summer Bible camp. Look at the boys poking a wounded locust on the sidewalk. But my history was biblical. It was the deed first, yes, but the thought—figuring out the ideas behind it. I named it. Evil. It was there from the beginning. The first man born into the world, Cain, murdered. Where did he learn it? Did he see it on television? Did he hear lyrics, "Kill, kill, kill"? No, it came from within. Where else? The disobedience of both mother and father. A brother that seemed to get God's approval over the offering of a lamb. Cain's own harvest set aside. No, that wasn't what God wanted. What's the matter with you, Cain? If you do well, you will be accepted. If not, you will not. And Cain, still angry, killed Abel in the field.

When the Lord asked Cain where his brother was—"What have you done? His voice cries to me from the ground. Now you are cursed. The earth will not let you till it. You will be a fugitive and a vagabond."

"My punishment is more than I can bear," Cain replied. "Anyone who sees me will kill me."

"Not so," God said, and marked Cain's forehead so others would know not to kill him.

What *others* were there? Wasn't it the beginning when there was no one else but Adam, Eve, and Cain? Maybe God had created others. Maybe they were the others to come. Maybe six thousand years ago, this new order, this new age, was imposed upon the millions of years of earth's history. Earth had pre-existed, had been destroyed, then was restored again. Shaped, unshaped, and shaped again. Maybe it had happened several times. More than several. But I was responsible only for the age in which I lived—not the mystery surrounding all the eras that had been. Yes, a minister could think that.

Or did God inject his brand of people among the tribes of people already living? Cain moved to Nod. He had a wife and a son, Enoch. He built a city called Enoch. His son, Enoch, had a son, Irad. Irad had a son, Mehujael. Mehujael had a son, Methusael. Methusael had a son, Lamech. And Lamech said to his wives, "I have killed a man."

One of Us

Was murder ingrained in the human heart? Was a longing for the knowledge of good and evil there too? But to have the knowledge of evil was to be implicated. It was to be in it. It was not to be separate. It was a pine nut in the ground. It could take root. It could be nurtured. It could be contorted. From outward causes, or sometimes just from within. What skewed a human mind to not leave it alone? To provoke the evil within? To align it to the power of evil in the world? I see. I want. I take.

But God himself killed. It was through the death of Jesus on the cross that salvation came. Jesus' death neutralized evil. Evil would bruise the heel of Christ on the cross. But Christ would bruise his head.

Satan, scorned, laughed at, mocked. Could he be real? As an energy force, certainly, but as a spiritual being? Someone creeping around the earth looking to add to his doomed kingdom?

How could I stand before my congregation and warn them of Satan? Why hadn't I done it before? It took one of my own congregation to bring it out in the open. To enact in the personage of Satan. To creep around neighborhoods with a fury, deciding who would die. Enter their houses and lord it over them, taking their life and masturbating over them, before or after they were dead? What was he thinking? What had gotten into the man? How could he live as a member of the congregation, as a leader in the congregation? How could he do these opposites?

The tiny cry of the snake haunted me. Snakes kept rodents in check. Why had I killed it? Probably just a brown snake, Roy said. He had seen them before.

God sent floods and storms and wiped nations out. He could hop over them. He could unload his hay wagon. He could bowl them over. He could stomp them out. And he did. He could warn. He could put the light on men and women. He could find the black cavern where the pine nut of evil was. It could grow. It could choke out resistance.

It could be developed. It could be dwelt on.

This snake I had in my hands.

42

Ralph Gheary
Anger

"How can you tolerate him?" I asked when Mark returned to the church. "I've known Tom a long time. He was on the committee that brought me here. I knew Tom before—"

"Before what? You're trying to tell me you knew him before he murdered, but you didn't."

"Listen to yourself, Ralph. I know you're shaken, but you're—"

"No, no. I listen to my wife cry. Her parents want her to come back to Elwood. We haven't been married a year. What am I supposed to do?" I felt expelled from the ministry by a man who wasn't worthy to touch the parking lot of the church, or even to lick the gravel at the side of the road.

"Why don't you both visit Zelda's parents?"

"I was just there for her grandmother's funeral," I answered. "I want to stay here. Zelda wants to stay. Hasn't Fout come into our bedroom and murdered us? Aren't we his victims also? Look what he has done to us. To our lives. You are older and have known more grief. We don't have children yet. We've hardly left the doors of the seminary. I want to bolt from church. I can hardly sit still in the pew, but I am staying here."

"You caused Thomas Fout grief when you visited him."

"He called you about it?"

Mark nodded.

"Isn't that what God's word is supposed to do?" I asked. "God is justice as well as mercy."

"Are you sure you don't want a leave of absence?
"I hardly got here."

43

Zelda Gheary
The E-mails

Ralph sent me an e-mail from my office in the church:

Zelda, they told me you would find the ministry boring. That I should look for a church girl, someone in seminary, someone who had it in her blood. But I loved you. You were flamboyant. A risk-taker. You flirted with me because I was in seminary. You thought you would tempt me. But you got caught, and loved me too. We went off to Christ Church in Buckholt. I was afraid it would cramp your style. After several church suppers in a row, we drove to Wichita for dinner. We drove to Kansas City. We drove to Topeka. Oklahoma City was not beyond reach. Maybe even Fort Worth. But now it has landed: our trouble. Thomas Fout was in the church we came to. He was a different parishioner. He sat quietly in church reviewing the murders he had committed while we were being welcomed by Reverend Cabot and the congregation. What could ever top this? I hope you haven't found it boring. I myself have committed several sins. I am here to confess to you, my lovely wife. I was unministerly in my meeting today with Thomas Fout. I was downright unchristian. I told him he could roast his toes in hell. He insisted he was a Christian and I insisted he was not. I was as arrogant as he was when he broke into houses and decided the fate of his victims. I am sending this e-mail so you will have hard evidence. He got the better of me. You can turn it into my advisor at seminary, Dr. Howard Edwards. The seminary can revoke my license to preach. You will no longer be a minister's wife. We can go to Rio and tango all night. We can sell cucumbers by the road.

—Ralph

Ralph, my lovely, I choose Rio. Wherever it is, it will have trouble matching the excitement we've had here. No, I am not bored, was not bored before the outbreak of the psycho killer in our own church. For some reason, I didn't fear boredom when I married you. Maybe it was intuition. I leave this e-mail so you will have hard evidence of how I flaunt my flamboyance, so unworthy of a minister's wife, in the face of such sorrow in our church in God's kingdom.

—Zelda

Zelda, Would you meet me for prayer? I'm in my office at church.

—Ralph

When I got to Ralph's office, I could tell he was grieving. He hadn't been through this before. How many had? It was difficult. I wanted to support Ralph. I needed support myself. I didn't want Mark going to the lake, leaving us alone at the church. Ralph and I prayed, trembling together as if standing before God at the judgment seat. We were judging ourselves, and in that act, maybe sparing ourselves some of the later shame. We sat trembling together as the horror passed over us. I thought of that dark night in Egypt in the book of Exodus when death passed through the streets.

44

Ralph Gheary
Another Trip to Jail

I came home furious from another visit to Wyatt. Thomas Fout had visitors when I was there. People wanted to know him. To write about him. To make a film about him. Can you image?

"People are drawn to that sort of thing," Zelda said.

"What sort of thing?"

"The deviant. The sensational."

"Is that what you call him?" I asked.

"He's been on the news. He's made press. Why do go back there? I thought you weren't going to see him again."

"I'm trying to take some of the pressure off Mark." I slumped on the cracked leather sofa we had brought back from Zelda's grandmother's house, my feet resting by the lion's feet.

45

Zelda Gheary
Forth Worth Museum

Ralph and I went to Fort Worth at Mark's insistence. We needed to get away—regain perspective. I wanted to see the Kimbell Art Museum. Ralph wanted time to brood.

Jacopo Bassano, Italian, 1510–1592, *Supper at Emmaus*: After the resurrection, Jesus sat with his disciples. There was Jesus with his hand on a loaf of bread. There was a dog with cat ears. A servant with some kind of fowl on a platter. There were cherries on the white tablecloth. Were they supposed to be spots of blood, reminiscent of the cross?

Duccio di Buoninsegna, Italian, 1278–1318, *The Raising of Lazarus*: The lovely Lazarus, mummified, a little green, looking at the crowd subdued. A man taken care of by his sisters, two mothers, after their own had died.

We ate in the museum café. We sat in the courtyard. We drove to the historic stockyards district. Ralph wanted to get back to Buckholt. As we walked, I saw his slight limp again. We would get up the next morning and drive back to Buckholt. We would be there by late afternoon. For the first time in our marriage, I felt I was not sufficient for him.

I wished Griselda Foster were alive. I could talk to her. There was something about my mother I could not bother with my *subworld*. There was a door I could not open and tell her of the inner place I lived.

I bought postcards of paintings in the museum shop. Among them were Giovanni Bellini's *Christ Blessing*, ca. 1500, and Annibale Carracci's,

Zelda Gheary: Forth Worth Museum

The Butcher's Shop, painted in the early 1580s. The latter was a graphic painting of two men splitting the carcasses. There was blood and brokenness. I hid it under the other postcards, hoping Ralph would not notice. He would call it inappropriate for a minister's wife.

Christ was an angelic sweetness. Christ was the slaughtered one. I knew I had to have redemption for my *subworld* drawings. What would it be?

By chance, I picked up a book, *Under Blue Cup*, by Rosalind Krauss, an art theorist. I began reading it in the car the next day, becoming absorbed as the open country passed along I-35. I think Ralph was lost in his own world because he let me read without commenting on my interest in the book.

The groundwork, the grid upon which to hang the process of art, was her subject. Krauss combined recovery from an aneurysm with a critique of twentieth century art: "abstract art jettisoned the earlier access to . . . meaning staked on . . . space behind the drumhead. Painters opposed this by seeing the drumhead itself as their theme." I recognized the voice of someone speaking to me in a way I could not speak to myself. I wanted to cry. It was a world I could not reach but knew was there. It was a voice from the privileged world where people lived a parallel life to mine. From Krauss, I understood the wall and ceiling of the second bedroom in our house could be a canvas. As I started to draw on the drumhead of the small room, which was now my workroom, I could use the ceiling as my theme. I could use the texture of the walls. It was not my drawings, but the intersection of vertical wall and horizontal ceiling that mattered. Had not Christ changed perception? Had he not upset the structure of the synagogue?

Krauss wrote that it was the rules that allowed for spontaneity. The rules were Ralph's ministry. The subject of heaven and hell. The strings that connected me to faith. The roster of hymns and sermons and Biblical passages. The horror beyond them. The abyss. The unspeakable suffering of eternity without Christ. I could turn new corners. I could see predicament in a new way.

Krauss discussed opposition as a paradigm for depth and verticality, a support that provided physical substance. Did I understand what she was saying? Could I transform it into my own process? Faith defined in terms that had nothing to do with the usual forms of faith. The support system in other terms than what I had seen. I closed the book. I closed my eyes and felt the momentum of the car over the road. O God, how wonderful this book was. I had a structure of what I was doing. I had been led home.

One of Us

Maybe Fout had searched for the same outreach of structure for his life. In these aphorisms, I could learn to continue. I could place Fout in theoretical constraints. Krauss kept making the statement "Who you are," as the bedrock of endeavor. My bedrock was Buckholt, Kansas, where I was a lowly minister's wife carrying the baggage of education in art history to which another course in another lecture hall had just been added.

46

Grace Cabot
Church Supper

The new wife of an old member called me. What did I think about the arrest of Thomas Fout? I took a moment to respond. I hoped that in the pause the new wife would understand she had not asked an appropriate question. But had it been inappropriate? Wasn't that what they all were thinking? But it was presumptuous for the woman to call. What irritated me? The woman's attitude. She took a position she hadn't earned. It was as if, by marrying the member of the church, she was in the longstanding position also. Because of a marriage and an arrest, we were friends and could talk personally. Privately. Intimately.

No, we weren't friends. But what was wrong with me? I was a minister's wife, open to all. I didn't have the right to what? Shun anyone? Even a new, bold wife who should have known it was not her business. I resisted the woman with minimal answers. Yes. No. We don't know. Pastor Cabot hasn't told me.

Finally the woman addressed my distance, "I didn't mean to bother you."

"I'm not free to talk about the Fouts. It isn't my place. I don't know much."

"If anyone would know—"

"I don't know what else there is to know at the moment. The Fout family is in shock. They're mourning. I don't know what else I can add that hasn't already been in the paper," I said briskly.

"Are you in the middle of something?"

"I'm fixing supper."

"I'm about to start also." The woman maneuvered me into another conversation. "Lured" was the word. Yes, by trickery, we were friends discussing meals. Should we exchange recipes?

"Ben's a fussy eater. You must know. He said he's eaten with your family."

I looked at the ceiling. I could hang up the phone while the woman was still talking. I could scream. How many years had the phone rung in the middle of what I was doing? How many times had I set my work aside? But I didn't have patience for this woman. "He ate with us several times after Catherine died," I said. There—I'd mentioned the first wife's name.

"I don't know how Ruth Fout holds up her head."

"She's not an accomplice."

"He's her husband. She's his wife."

"They're divorced."

"How could she not be involved? How could she not know? Did she never find anything when she was cleaning? How many years had he hidden his victims' belongings?"

"Mrs. Fout had no idea what he'd done—it was before she knew him."

"Not all of the murders—"

"Most of the murders were committed before they married."

"Yes, but you'd think she would be aware of the baggage he had. You know he kept some of the belongings of his victims—driver's licenses—in the tree house where his children had played—he would go out there and look at them—"

"I don't think it's my business to think about it."

"But he wanted to see your husband. The paper said so—"

"Yes, my husband goes to see him as his pastor—"

"Your husband doesn't share with you?"

"What passed between Mark and Thomas is between them." I said goodbye and hung up the phone.

A church supper once a month had been part of the routine for years. Mark canceled the first one after Fout's arrest. But then he didn't see why they shouldn't continue. Maybe they were needed, now more than anytime.

Grace Cabot: Church Supper

Fout's sentencing was coming. Maybe there would be closure and we could move on. Maybe I was dreaming.

Others were at the church when we arrived. George and Harriet Weldon oversaw the mechanics of the dinner. Mildred Keller, the church secretary, and Fred, her husband, were there also. Sam and Molly Stanton, together with Ralph and Zelda Gheary, set up tables that Molly was covering with a cloth on which the covered dishes would be set. Then she sat her own macaroni in the center of the long table. I left Mark and went to join Molly, placing my chicken bake next to Molly's.

Harriet adjusted several covered dishes, moving napkins to the other side of the knives and forks. Mark stood talking to the men and their wives. The older children were in their groups. The younger children were in theirs, or standing by their parents. A stray wife—her husband talking to another. Beth Saith, Roy's wife, their daughter, and two boys had just arrived.

I talked to Beth about the way the new wife wanted to be included.

"You're looking tired, Grace," Molly said.

Edna Fraiser came from the kitchen. "I think she'll hold up," she said to Molly, as though I were a malfunctioning tractor that might not make it through the season.

I had worn my navy blue suit skirt, but I replaced the suit jacket with a sweater I had purchased several weeks ago. My flat shoes with rounded toes were serviceable. My shoulder-length hair was held back by a ribbon. My nose was straight and my mouth thin. I was the pastor's wife. My husband could handle whatever happened.

Mark came to me and put his hand on my back. It was a family night. I knew Mark wanted me to stay by him. I held out my hand for Clare, but she wanted to stay with the Saiths because she was friends with their daughter. Fellowship hall was quieter than usual. There were probably thirty people out of the sixty who usually came.

"We have a church supper the third Wednesday evening of every month," Mark said. "I see no reason to change it. Let's open in prayer. Dear Lord, see us through this evening. We have been hit. Guide us." I could hear the phone in Mark's office through the prayer. "Sometimes faith is a war," he continued. "The enemy has walked among us. Our church has been a refuge for a murderer. It finally spit him out by his own doing. Be with the Fout family. Be with Thomas Fout. We'll talk more of this later. For now, we'll eat and have fellowship. Amen."

The conversation was muted as the line moved along the table. Molly Stanton wiped her tears. I had heard the sniffles of others during the prayer. I wanted to cry also. I felt conflicted. It was our first church dinner without Ruth and Thomas Fout.

I continued to hear Mark talk as I stood beside him. It was warfare that didn't look like war. It was an unseen war. No, it was open war. Children were being lost to drugs, alcohol, and violence. Our congregation harbored sins. A man approved for the presidency of the congregation of Christ Church, Thomas Fout, had harbored sins. No, he had *neighbored* sins.

"My neighbor said, 'I've always thought there were creeps in church.'"

I felt like I was hearing only parts of the conversations. Or was I in church listening to Mark in the pulpit? I wasn't sure. Was he? No, we were waiting in line to take a plate.

It was a central message for the Christian. It should be. Jesus was the way, the truth, the life. No man came to the Father but by him. How could that message be overlooked? Ignored? For those not raised in the faith, it was a message that sounded ridiculous. How could I speak about it to children? I remembered hesitating before I spoke to Clare. Rehearsing the message. God lived someplace we couldn't go. But he made a way for us to be with him. We had sinned by turning away from him by our disobedience. God killed his Son and took his blood and covered us so that when he looked down on us he saw the blood of his Son smeared on us. I had been sweating when I finished. How could I say this to Clare? To anyone?

Mark was talking to someone else behind him. I took his arm and pulled him to the serving table when we were next in line to help ourselves to the food.

I was quiet during the supper.

Later, when Clare was working on her homework in her room and Mark and I were alone, I spoke: "I'm stopped everywhere I go. Someone always knows who I am. What do I think? What will the church do? Who would have thought? What were we going to do? How will we hold our heads up? What did we do? Harbor a criminal? Yes, that's what we've done."

"It's all right, Grace. You feel exposed."

"I am exposed."

Grace Cabot: Church Supper

"You're happiest when you are unnoticed. That's why you like the front row. The privacy of it. You're removed from the congregation. It's your act of rebellion," Mark said.

"Why didn't you know?" I asked. "Maybe you weren't praying enough."

"I pray for all the members of our church," Mark answered. "I never knew."

"There always was something creepy about him."

"You never said anything."

"I didn't like him—and Ruth seemed illusive. There was something in her held back."

"You're angry. You feel defrauded."

"Don't you?"

"Are you arguing about him again?" Clare was in the kitchen then. How much had she heard?

"What do they say at school?" Mark asked.

"My friends are sorry it happened to us. They wonder if we were scared. They ask what his children must have thought, remembering all those years they slept in his house."

"What do you say?"

"No, I wasn't scared. He wouldn't hurt anyone in church."

I was glad that was clear to her, though I wasn't so sure myself. I wasn't sure of anything after Thomas Fout's arrest.

There was another phone call, another news reporter, another Christian radio station from everywhere in the country. Television cameras, visitors in his church, drive-bys came to see the place. I stayed at the church to answer the phone and help Mildred. Ralph and Zelda were there also.

I heard Mark answer questions. There were questions he couldn't answer. He didn't know what had gone wrong. There were things he could not explain. Thomas Fout found sin in his life. What was the nature of sin? Forgetting God. Ignoring the Holy Spirit. Forgetting God was worse than murder? I knew what they were saying, though I couldn't hear the other side of the conversation. I looked at Mildred, who shrugged her shoulders.

I listened to Mark stammer. God is righteous. His righteous nature has to judge sin. I heard another pause. Then Mark started into the gospel again. But we were separated from him. God wanted us to be with him. He had to get us on board with him, but he couldn't. His justice wouldn't let us.

He had to have righteousness. His justice wouldn't let us coexist with him. He judged sin in the person of Christ. If we accepted Christ, he would use that propitiation for us. He could accept us in Christ, on whom he had laid the judgment for sin.

There it was—Mark could say it without sending the listener running the other way, eventually screaming into another religion.

What if Mark said to the cameras, "Satan comes to confuse, to bind, torture, kill?" Everyone would laugh, I thought. The camera would be tuned off. The cameramen, the reporters, the vans would go away. That's what I wanted to happen. When would the mess go away? The mess given to us by a loving God I had trusted.

My father would not have been able to face anyone like Thomas Fout. He had sat in the parlor, his study, and talked to people about Christian issues that were . . . What? Gentle. Was that the word? I had not known, or cared to know, there were people like Thomas Fout. My father had protected me. What a cocoon I had been in, and I wanted back into it.

47

Mark Cabot
Concern

In the afternoon, I had a visit from a husband and wife. Their lives had not gone well. They were burdened by disappointment, anger, and debt. They were thinking of separation.

"Wouldn't it be easier?" the husband asked. An apartment for one of them. More expense, I answered. The children divided between them. It would be like leaving their front doors unlocked, I said. Their separation would lead the way to more debt. After we talked, I prayed, opening up their losses before the Lord. I asked them to consider the consequences before they made their decision. I would see them again.

There were days I came home heavy-hearted, and Grace would have a meal prepared for the man who heard everything. And I felt I had. I knew what to do with broken couples, but this issue of Thomas Fout opened up an area I had not been in—blatant evil and Fout's ability to sit in church with murder in his lap. Had my sermons been ineffective? Trying to separate the people from evil was like trying to divide water. I felt I didn't know much, but Jesus called the fishermen to his side—those who handled nets, who knew the sea—though he would have called the priests if they had followed him.

What made a man kill? Grace listened to me agonize over the conflict.

Sometimes someone stopped us on the street, or in a parking lot, or at a restaurant or in line at Walmart. What made Fout cross the line that seared his conscience? What stop-gap was not there? What anger backlogged in him until he broke into a murderous rage? Or worse—what if he was cool and calculated? What provoked him, goaded him? What made him lash out? Did he know the people? Had they slighted him? Had they done him an injustice? How long had he thought of it before he performed the deed? How long did Cain, the first murderer, think? Did it also come on him as a sudden urge? What made most people pass by the act of murder when it entered their thoughts, if evil was buried somewhere in all of us?

How long had Fout hungered for power? Thirsted over it. How long had he wanted the power of life and death before he killed?

I woke in the night thinking of Christ on the cross. Scripture says he was disfigured on the cross (Isaiah 52:14), that he was marred beyond anything that looked human. He had stepped into our evil—into all the inhumane acts we could commit against each other. He had taken it head on.

Grace, my wife, slept beside me, turning once in a while. I thought about her in the dark. I could see her form in the light of the clock radio. Once, from deep in her sleep, I heard a sigh of distress.

I had recognized her signs of stress. She snapped at Clare over nothing. I felt the stiffness of her body. She seemed thinner. Narrower. But I could rely on her. I would be with her the rest of my life. I remembered the comfort of that thought. There would be no change. She and Clare would be with me. After Fout, I had thought I could never be sure of anything again, but I was sure of this. Grace and Clare would be beside my bed as I passed into the Lord's arms. Maybe Clare's husband and children would be there too, if I lived that long. The child we lost would be there. We would wait for Grace and Clare and for the grandchildren I might not live long enough to know. We all would be returned to the wonder of God's love, where we had stayed as close as possible in this life. Tessa Margaret Cabot. Would she have a nametag so I would know her? Would she have continued to grow? Would she be a woman I would not recognize? No, there was no male or female in heaven. But she would be a person I would know. We all would know one another. Would we all stand around? What was heaven like? What would we be like there? How many questions for which I did not have answers? Why was I given so few answers? What was I doing?

Go, be a minister, God seemed to say, but I can't tell you how to get there, or what it will be like. Just act like you have the answers in this hard, practical world that can walk right past the living God and not even notice.

Mark Cabot: Concern

In this hard world where the enemy hacks away at the map and tries to distort it.

It was a story of taking a trip to a place I didn't know for sure was there, but on one map, the map I decided to follow, the Bible, it was there, and though some told me it was not, I was going anyway.

I remembered those I had counseled in my pastorate. They left my office angry. They weren't going to believe in a God who took their child, or their parent, or who let the Nazi's run the world for a while. There was no God. There was no—what?—nothing?

When I woke, Grace was not in bed.

Maybe she was already in the kitchen. Maybe Clare had called her. Clare had continued to have nightmares. It was the aftershock of the Fout affair. We would never be free from it. Just like we were never free of the loss of Tessa. There were events that marked a turn in the road that would be there always.

48

Ralph Gheary
Free Will

"We have free will," I told the youth group, "Some of us use it in the wrong way." I continued to talk to the group. They were in high school. It was a tough crowd.

In my office at the church after the youth group meeting, I looked through my books to have something to do with the helplessness I felt. I had not taken the time to organize them as yet. There was something in my position at Christ Church that didn't feel permanent. I looked over the books and picked one out, *The Spiritual Teachings of Marcus Aurelius*.

"What is a name? Just sound. An echo." I browsed. Aurelius had been wrong. A name was everything. Just ask Thomas Fout.

"To have a good name in a world like this was meaningless." Still, I did not agree. I'd always felt a leadership. In boys' games. In sports. I had attracted a pretty wife. I had garnered prizes. I had flown through seminary. I was in touch with the world. I talked to Dr. Edwards almost as a friend. Now I was riding second seat to a member of the congregation who had taken the church on patrol.

49

Mark Cabot
Several Visits

I visited Tom in jail several times. I was a minister. I had to follow the same rules for everyone. Fout continued to ask if he could meet privately with me to talk. He asked that Ralph Gheary not come to the jail anymore. I tried to explain that he was new in the ministry, but Thomas said he would refuse to see him if he came again. We sat in a separate room at a table looking at one another, hearing other voices in the main visiting room. Some bickering, some blame, some tears. Some looking at the man they knew was the murderer. I was glad a guard was at the window. I wished there was a curtain.

It was a while before I realized what Thomas wanted: my endorsement.

This was a man who transgressed—who crossed the line into the other—who was where he should not be—who did what he should not do—who took their lives into his hands and extinguished them—who turned family members of the victims to bitterness—who touched evil—who had it in his hands.

"You've been playing with the serpent," I told Thomas. "You want me to defend you? To sit with you in court to give you whatever respectability you can muster? Are you even ashamed?"

"I know I have done wrong," Thomas said. "I know I have ruined lives."

"You also know Kansas revoked the death penalty during the years you murdered. Then when it was reinstated, you ceased your murdering."

"I've carried this burden for years."

"I preach forgiveness and grace, but this is beyond that," I said. "This is something I don't know how to handle."

I had to get hold of myself. I was using Thomas as a confessor, telling him I felt unworthy, unable to handle the conundrum he presented. Further, the situation brought up other, less clear issues. Was Fout a Christian? By all accounts, yes. I heard his profession of faith in Jesus Christ. He was baptized. He had been a member of the congregation for over two decades. I had talked to the previous minister, who had baptized his children. He knew them. He vouched for them. Now Thomas turned up as a murderer. I heard his confession of murder.

Did Fout lose his salvation through the act of murder? Was murder more important, more deadly than the other sins? But God was forgiveness. The gifts were not taken back. The only unforgivable sin was unbelief. For that there was no remedy.

What puzzlement Thomas had brought—what anger, anguish, loss.

50

Ralph Gheary
The Sentencing

Zelda sat next to me at the sentencing of Thomas Fout. Mark and Grace Cabot sat on the other side of us next to other members of the congregation who were there for support. Fout would be in the state prison at Wyatt for the rest of his life.

Afterwards, the families of the victims had their turn to speak to Fout. They told him of the pain they had carried for decades. Some were unable to speak. Other spoke with trembling. Still others were resolute with anger. They spurted out the hollowness left by the murdered member of their family. I felt the tension that filled the room. Many of the families left when it was Fout's turn to address the court.

51

Mark Cabot
A Prayer to Wash the Church

Fout had nearly convinced me that he repented, but there on the news, Fout was talking again to a reporter. He had picked out his next victim, but wouldn't say who it was. Fout had not repented. He had teased a flaw. He had listened to its tune until he couldn't get it out of his head.

I had driven many times to the state prison at Wyatt, some sixty-five miles north of Buckholt on I-35. From time to time, I was part of a group of ministers who held services there. But I had not been to visit one of my own congregation.

Fout was upset when I saw him. Ruth was going to sell their house at an auction. He had not been a part of that decision. She had divorced him. She could do what she wanted with the house.

"That's what happens when you commit murder. You give up your rights as an individual. You murdered yourself in a way."

"I can't even order a pizza," he responded.

"Several members of the congregation visited Ruth," I continued. "They asked her to return to church. To stay in the choir. We all signed a letter in agreement and gave it to her."

"I have another confession," Fout said.

He looked stiff behind the glass. The harsh overhead light glared on his face.

"What is it?" I asked

Mark Cabot: A Prayer to Wash the Church

"It's something I didn't tell the court at the hearing—a detail I left out. I brought one of the bodies into church before I dumped it."

I looked at Fout. "Don't tell me who it was," I said, rising from my chair.

I turned abruptly and left the prison. There was something coiled inside me. I felt it strike. It was something I had to carry with me. It was something I had no one to tell.

I returned to the church that night when everyone was gone. In the dark, I prayed that God would wash the church of the acts of Thomas Fout.

For what purpose had evil come so close?

52

Zelda Gheary
Swallow a Camel

There were warnings of artifice in the Bible. Of copying. Of similitude. Of making likeness. "Neither shall you make any other like it, after the composition of it: it is holy."[1] Whosoever compounds any like it—I had to stay away from getting close, yet my *subworld* had to reveal the truth. I stewed. I fretted. I was torn one way and another. How much like hell this must be. No rest or certainty: "You blind guides, who strain at a gnat and swallow a camel."[2]

Was I wrong to copy the images of hell? Wasn't I creating? I ran into my art for refuge, for solace.

"Then the tabernacle of the congregation shall set forward with the camp of the Levites in the midst of the camps; as they encamp, so shall they set forward, every man in his place."[3] I liked the rhythm of that passage. I read it several times. Could the rhythms of words be in the lines of a drawing of a *subworld*?

"Get out of the Old Testament for a while," Ralph recommended.

I saw him limp slightly as he left the room. It was from an old injury. Sometimes when he was tired or stressed, he would favor his left leg.

---

1. Exod 30:32.
2. Matt 23:24.
3. Num 2:17.

53

Mark Cabot
District Meeting of Ministers

I liked to be in church. I had liked the Sunday school lessons as a boy. It was a desire I had—to be there. Later, there were harder things to consider: the puzzles, the quandaries of man's relationship to God, the essence of God, and my own despondence in the face of my certainty in Christ. I had persistent thoughts about belief—accountability—the responsibility to faith. I felt it was a calling. There was nothing else I wanted to do but to help people. I would write sermons, talk about God each week, shepherd a flock. I liked to think about the quandaries. They enticed me. They excited me. They persuaded me to become a minister. I felt it was the evidence of my belief: I wanted to shepherd those who wanted to be shepherded.

Saint Augustine. The Bible. Martin Luther. The missals. The text. The physical space. The place. It was where I belonged. I liked the explanation, the defense of Scriptures to those having trouble believing. To say words of comfort at death. To explain heaven. To explain the unexplainable. To make clear what was clear to no one, not even myself. I wanted to be in the business of eternity. To help people through life. To hear oppositional ways chaffing against one another. To ponder. Meditate. Think on the things there were to think on. To be with people in marriage and baptism. To suffer with them. To rejoice. To usher their souls into heaven. What was more important than that?

I remembered being scoffed by my uncles for not joining in on the hard work. The lifting. The fieldwork. The repairing of cars. Machinery.

Men's work. I held back. I didn't feel comfortable with mechanics. I was not good at fixing machines. I wanted to fix thoughts, to understand paradox. That was my field.

I remember my first awkward sermons at the Lutheran seminary. At least I wasn't overly confident like others I had seen. I felt my way along. My wife and I had endured poverty. Grace had not opened catalogs. She had not gone shopping without her list.

I continued my visits with Tom Fout. But there were questions not so easily resolved. Would Fout go to heaven? That always was the question. Christ was his Lord. But Fout was a murderer. There was no room for murderers in heaven. You know that no murderer has eternal life abiding in him.[1]

Often, I felt invisible. I had time to read. I took another call from Dr. Cole, the former minister of the church, who was retired, frail, and not able to bear much of it. I watched cars go by the church, never looking, never stopping, never wondering what the church was doing. I prayed for them, and still they passed, oblivious to who the church was, what it was doing, how it could have soothed their way. Yes, they lived their quiet lives while Satan ravaged the world and the people in it, convincing them Christ did not die on the cross. He did not rise from the tomb. He had a wife and children—progeny somewhere in the south of France. People traveled there looking for clues. Christ was a imposter. The church had made up his resurrection. The gospel smeared with doubt.

They had their shelf where they stayed, their dock above the waters.

What could I say?

I made notes for a sermon, or a talk, or what? "There was a little city, and a few men within it; and there came a great king against it, and besieged it, and built great bulwarks against it."[2]

He was one of us. Neighbor, husband, father, compliance officer, dogcatcher, president of the congregation of Christ Church. There were rumors, but none guessed a murderer was so close. If he could have been

---

1. 1 John 3:15.
2. Eccl 9:14.

Mark Cabot: District Meeting of Ministers

brain-injured, or severely abused, it would have been easier. If there was an x-factor in serial killers to blame. But Fout's murders seemed to have a natural progression. He started first with dogs "territorial and vicious," he said in a television interview. He made people obey the ordinances of the city while breaking a few himself. The dogs suffered too when they were cornered, caught. Bound, tortured, killed. The love of a secret life, of power, of control, of his right to patrol and execute his own judgments. Judas infiltrated the inner circle of Christ's disciples for the purpose of betrayal. Did Fout take our self-righteousness and blow it to bits (as if the Nazis didn't teach us enough) so we might know what we are capable of even inside the church? A Boy Scout leader who *let loose*, who brutalized, overstepped. *How many people do I have to kill until I get the attention I deserve?* We do not know who we are. We do not know our human nature, *the old man*, the neighbor within us. Fout was in the army, installed alarm systems. He was in law enforcement. He had a thirst for publicity.

There was no mystery, no secret to be found. It was given. It was there—our independence from blame and excuse. It was the truth we keep jailed: how a thin line divided what we did openly and what we kept locked in the prison of ourselves.

Open the Bible anywhere. Just anywhere. There is a psalm, a word or words hoisting me. Unbelief was the unforgivable sin. Unacceptance of God's plan of salvation.

The bishop arrived late in the day for another visit. Did he sense my depression? Did he see the black cloud I saw? No, he asked me to speak at the district meeting.

"How are you going to handle it?" he asked.

"With the truth."

"What is the truth?"

"I don't know," I said.

"We can say what we think as long as it aligns with Scripture. But even Scripture can be twisted—as if we weren't in enough of a muddle. We're in harm's way every day. We're in danger. There're bigger problems than what we've got. The terrorists will keep coming. Are we too smeared with our own trouble to meet it? Our congregations can move to the next church. We have a declining membership. We are troubled with trouble. We have come to the end of the road, but there's always a road at the end of the road. We'll never reach the end. Not in Christ."

"I feel like I'm in a bag of fuzz," I said. "It's all one mess I can't separate. I can't start anything different. I only can do what I've always done—pray. And what would be my prayer? I come to you, Jesus, at the end of my rope. I cry out to you. Why did this happen? Do you know your kingdom looks ridiculous? I am prostrate on the floor. I am made of dust."

I spoke at the district meeting of ministers as the bishop requested.

I opened in prayer: "I come to you, Lord, in this humiliation. One of my flock has murdered ten people. I'm sure you have his name on record. I'm sure you have known all along. But we are now just finding out about it. His arrest is a relief to Buckholt, I can assure you, but it is humbling to us. To be honest, a devastation.

"One of your sheep, Thomas Fout, who is counted in my flock, a member of my congregation for years, has committed murder. Not just one murder. Not an accidental or a *justifiable* murder of someone who had harmed him, raped his daughter, beat his mother in front of him, scarred him for life, ripped to shreds the understanding of family. No, it seems to me, he chose his victims at random, watched them, and executed his judgment on them. A faithful and prominent member of the church, not just someone who came now and then, Christmas and Easter, and left a dollar. No, he was a significant member. President of the congregation, as a matter of fact. I am at a loss. What is there to say? A murderer in our midst. Right in the middle."

I was getting lost in prayer. I said, amen. I heard others say, amen, glad the cloudy prayer had ended. But as I continued talking, it was still prayer. "Thomas Fout used the church computer to write a letter to the newspaper. I'm sure you are aware of the situation. The newspaper ran an article. They felt, twenty-five years later, that he wasn't around. Fout reminded them that he was—right here on our church computer. He left clues. Maybe he wanted to be caught. Maybe all those years of listening to sermons, of sitting in meetings, finally brought his murders to the surface to be exposed. He was a church member, a believer. To the best of my knowledge he was—I heard his profession of faith on more than one occasion. I can't tell you how dumbfounded we are. How flabbergasted. We are at a loss for what to say. Our faces are red. I feel like we have been caught also. Apprehended. What is our crime? My crime? His crime?

Mark Cabot: District Meeting of Ministers

I am at odds here. I am coming apart. How can I face the cameras that continue to hound me? The jeers? The laughter behind the scenes of those who do not believe in Christ—who do not believe in church? This is another reason they should not come to church. Murderers are there. And surely they are. Or were. I would remind you that Cain, the first-born, murdered his brother because of jealousy. I cannot get Cain off my mind. Ideas circle and circle. Ideas fly everywhere. I try to find mercy for Fout. But God is justice also. He does not allow evil in his presence. Worse are the personal implications. Am I Abel, killing Cain to get rid of him? I will remind you, God, of the long line of your people. Hardly any of them behaved themselves. You asked Abraham to murder Isaac, his son. You do not need to be reminded that you, yourself, put your own Son on the cross. If ever there was a stumbling block to belief—a God who murders his own Son? What is the meaning of that? I have heard that more than once. I couldn't believe in a religion like that. What do we say of Christianity? How do you make sense of the warring factions, the denominations that do not agree on essential tenets? How do you reconcile?"

"I'm getting off-track here. To return to the point: How do I face the cameras, the news media, the ones in my own congregation? The embarrassment? How could we have had him in our midst and not known? What do we say to those who laugh? O Lord, where will I get strength not to tremble before them? To defend the faith—your faith, I remind you. This is more about my embarrassment as a pastor. I should have had discernment. I should have known. I should have been able to tell, if I was doing my job as a minister. Did I pray and receive warning from you and let it go unnoticed? There is a chance—in a dream, in something Fout said or did that flashed a warning. I can't remember.

"No, to get to the main point—to get back on track—have mercy on Thomas Fout and his family. Have mercy on all that is before them. Give them strength. Give them a peace beyond understanding."

My prayer became most of the meeting. I had prepared a short talk to give to the district meeting of ministers, but as I continued to pray, they got up from their chairs and gathered around me. They laid their hands upon my shoulders. I felt like I would come apart, explode, rip at the seams, at the cracks in my foundation. They prayed one after the other, then all at once. I heard their many voices, the accumulated prayers, the power. I felt my legs grow weak. I felt them help me to a chair. The prayers continued until I could stand again.

54

Zelda Gheary
A Recurring Dream

I was troubled by a recurring dream in which I saw the weaving of string fires bordering a field at night. I thought it was a farmer burning off brush to prevent a prairie fire in a drought. I saw firebrands from a bucket of live coals. I saw someone taking his tongs, placing them where he willed, when the world felt hot and dry enough to ignite.

I wrote the words "prairie fire" on my *subworld* drawing as I worked the next day.

55

Grace Cabot
Daughters

I had lost a daughter. I had seen other children die. Then there was Thomas Fout. I could not understand why God had allowed him to live while my small daughter died. Was it resentment I felt swimming in my thoughts? A resentment I could not face. I held back part of myself. I knew I could not fully trust God. I did not sing as loudly as I could in church. I did not pray as fervently. As a child, on the farm, I had held back a little feed I should have thrown to the chickens, throwing it instead into the tall grass where the hens would have a harder time getting it. No, God was someone I had to keep at arm's length. I was a minister's wife. I measured carefully. I did not expect a lot from God, especially children other than Clare. I knew there would be none. Clare was already twelve. How the years had flown, I thought in the night, or as I visited with my sisters. I had to be on guard. I could lead prayer at dinner. I could speak of God, but there was a distance between me and the God my husband served. This latest event was just like God. Just like something he would do: *Let them have a killer in their congregation for twenty-five years so they could be mocked.* Were we blind? Deaf? Undiscerning? How could that be? How could we let that happen? We were glad for our congregation. For all those who paid tithe, who attended church, who brought covered dishes to church suppers, who came to whatever the church offered. Who parked their car in the parking lot on Sunday mornings. No, don't share rides. We wanted the lot to look as full as possible. We observed churches on Sunday mornings as we drove to our own church, noting which were prosperous. Which were not. Which were struggling for members. Which were going through a crisis. Why did I notice the ones in trouble? Why didn't the prosperous ones come to mind first?

Now we were in the throes of struggle. How many members would we lose?

How would it affect Clare? What would the children say to her at school?

From the beginning, I told Clare that Thomas Fout had been arrested for murder. I wanted Clare to know that a man in our church had done something terrible, and that he was arrested and would not be back in our church—ever. He was going to prison for the rest of his life. He would have to sit in a small room and think about the terrible things he had done. He would be sorry—very sorry. He had hurt people. He had hurt them terribly, and he would not be back. That's what happened to someone who had done something terrible. He would have to sit by himself and think. He would one day face God, face to face, and have to answer why he had done it. He had all his time in prison to think about it. Maybe he would have to face the people he had murdered. How terrible that would be. That was his punishment. Not to be in his house ever again. Not to sit in church or be with others. To know that his family was shamed. That they could hardly hold up their heads around others. It was terrible—terrible.

Maybe the children would say something to Clare about him being in her father's church, about her father not knowing it, about them being surprised—shocked, horrified actually—that he had been in their church. But God loved everyone, even murderers, though he hated the acts the murderers committed. And there was forgiveness in Christ. Christ could forgive him, yes, and they could too, in time. But it was so sudden. They were so disgusted that they were implicated. Yes, that was it. They were part of it because they had harbored a murderer in their flock. They hadn't known he was the man who bound, tortured, killed. To think of it, just to think of it, made my skin crawl. I had sat next to him. I had been in his house. To pick something up. To drop something off. It was our job to be shepherds to the Fout family, as it always had been. No matter what happened. Only now it was harder. Much harder. It was something I didn't want to do, though I hardly realized it yet. I thought of the children who had lived with him. The woman who had slept in bed with him. Had they bowed their heads in prayer before meals? Had they had confession? Had they had any idea? Had he tossed in his sleep? Had he spoken? Had he let anything slip? Where had he said he was those nights he was prowling for a victim? Did the vaguest suspicion ever cross her mind?

I had to remember I was talking to Clare. I couldn't let myself go astray. I couldn't let my thoughts get into the conversation. How depraved Thomas Fout was. How morbid the situation. Everyone was overly concerned. Preoccupied until it was all we could think of.

How I longed for Tessa. Mark had not understood.

The following Sunday morning we drove to the apartment where Ruth Fout was staying. Mark went up to the door for her. She was ready and followed him to the car. She sat in the backseat with Clare. We were quiet all the way to Christ Church. We walked into the church silently. Mark went to his office to put on his robe. Clare joined her friends. Ruth and I went to the front row where we waited for church to begin.

56

Mark Cabot
The Saiths'

I knew Grace didn't want to come to the Saiths' cabin, but I needed her there. She would do what I asked, even if she didn't want to, though I knew she also had an aversion to staying by herself at night in the parsonage.

I felt her restlessness as she fixed supper.

"Would you like me to drive you back home?"

"No," Grace answered. "Do you want us to leave?"

"No, I want you here," I told her. "I just have to think. I want to hear you stirring in the cabin."

After supper, Grace walked with Clare to a cabin down the road. There was a girl there she knew. They would play until dark.

Thomas Fout could have been injured as a child. He could have been abused. He could have been put together differently. He could have been evil. What made him murder? Had he longed for control over people's lives? He went into bedrooms—private places with chests of drawers of socks and underwear and personal belongings. He killed his victims in their own rooms. In their own beds. Hurting them. Binding them. How could he do that?

Mark Cabot: The Saiths'

I believed the Bible. Then I had to believe that Satan, an enemy of God, looked for those he could deceive—those he could use—could stamp with himself. He wanted to harm. Kick up dust. Provoke. Discourage. Kill.

"You are going to see him again," Grace said later that evening when Clare was asleep. "He has sucked you in."

"I'm committed to visit him in prison."

Grace pushed the book I was reading to the floor. "I've thought about Thomas Fout until I can't think anymore."

I drew her to the screened porch, where we listened to the rain that had started to fall. I felt her shivering when I put my hand on her back. It was as if the rain had penetrated her skin and was running down her spine.

57

Ralph Gheary
Get Him off My Mind

There were those who understood immediately and reacted. There were others who experienced a delayed reaction—men and women who continued to come to the church to talk through the crisis. They had to discuss it, come to a point. I listened as they talked. They had been asked about Fout. How could a church member answer? What a whammer: Fout, the mass-murderer president of the council on which they served. They had sat with him in church. The question kept returning. How could they be so blind? Deluded? Had they liked him? Hadn't he been a stickler? Yes, but he'd been elected president of the governing council of the church. What a hoot. What an unbelievable situation. What would they do? How to recover? Put the embarrassment behind them? Face the public? Explain to their children how a murderer could be in their midst? How could they trust others again when someone so normal could be so abnormal? Should they elect a new president? Yes, they needed a leader.

Who could follow Thomas Fout? Hadn't he been the ultimate council president? Was this a first in church history? No. There had been worse.

Had the Holy Spirit finally gotten hold of him and made him send a disk that could be traced? Hadn't Fout showed his hand? Was he tired of hiding? Did he want to confess?

I had to get my mind off Fout and back to the church where I worked.

58

Mark Cabot
The Church Election

I asked the council to nominate several people for the congregation to vote on for their president. We prayed about the election. I decided to hold it in two weeks—on communion Sunday—when there was a sense of community and gratefulness for the cup of salvation.

Roy Saith was the first member nominated, but he refused. He said he was afraid of his rage against Thomas Fout. He had been with him on committees. He had been irritated by his authoritarian manner, his attitude of superiority. What did he have to say? A dogcatcher. A man who measured his neighbor's grass with a ruler.

Roy was a Christian, but he said he did not feel like one. Thomas had provoked something unchristian in him.

"As he has in all of us," I answered.

Roy was my friend. I used his cabin whenever I wanted. Our children played together. Roy and Beth stayed in the hospital with us when Tessa was sick. Our wives led the women's prayer ministry at church.

But Roy insisted that he did not want to be nominated. He continued to share his thoughts. I didn't know how to stop him. How could he pray for a man who'd had his hands around throats, choking off air? Then letting the victims breathe. Letting them choke their way back to life. Letting them think they would live. Then stopping their air again—slowly. So slowly that they would know what was happening. To prolong their fear. Their anguish.

I put my hand out to Roy to indicate he'd said enough, but he continued.

He suspected there were more victims. Maybe some of them would never be found. Roy could have strangled Fout himself, thinking of a woman alone in a house when he entered.

"That's enough, Roy," I said. "We've all had these thoughts. But we need to move on as a congregation." The church council agreed.

Roy was more of a help to me than Ralph Gheary, the assistant minister, a young man just out of seminary who sat next to me. Roy had thought about the ministry but had joined Saith Construction, his father's company, and took it over when his father retired.

I was used to explaining. To feeling fragile. To facing a hard job. Answering big questions for little pay. I laughed about it sometimes. Other times it bit. Especially when Roy came driving up in his new diesel truck that cost what I made in a year.

"If you had been president of the congregation, this wouldn't be as embarrassing."

"I work," Roy said, "and sometimes we spend the weekend at the lake."

Roy left the meeting. Why had I let momentary jealousy and bitterness cloud our relationship? No, it wasn't momentary. I had to ask forgiveness. I was mad at God and took it out on Roy because I had a harder time than he did, or thought I did.

That was Roy's problem, I thought angrily. He had an easier way than I did. He had not lost a child. He had not been tested.

I guided the church council through the rest of the meeting. We would move toward healing. It was our choice.

The nominations continued. Charles Zack. Chase McConnell. Jack Kester. Sandra Gilmore.

We held an election on communion Sunday for president of the congregation. The vote went to Kester, who also served as head of the maintenance committee. Kester spoke to the congregation after the election. His voice broke several times, but he was able to continue. I saw others crying in the congregation as he spoke. How long would it take for us to recover?

Several families had left the congregation. They told me beforehand that they could not continue to be members of the church. They could not be affiliated with the church where a murderer was a member.

They were running from themselves, I thought angrily. They had to run. They were sorry to leave. Goodbye. Their member transfer papers came from another church. Others who I had not seen before showed up. I didn't trust them. Onlookers. They just wanted to see where the Fout family had worshipped.

    I went to Roy Saith as everyone was leaving church that morning. I offered my hand. He took it.

59

Grace Cabot
A Consideration

How he had bound them? What had they felt? What was it like to be strangled? I could imagine their terror. I continually thought about Thomas Fout. It was all about him.

I was the wife of a minister. My father had been a minister. I was used to church. I met Mark Cabot at Bethany College, a Lutheran seminary. We dated several years before we married. After we married, Mark started as an assistant minister in a small church in another part of Kansas. I had a degree in theology. Before we had children, I had a ministry to the elderly. I had talked with my father in the rectory. I could think. I held my own with my brothers. My older brother, Edward, had left the ministry after his wife divorced him. He led a Bible study for divorced men but could never return to the pulpit. My younger brother, Philip, had a small church in another neighborhood. A Pentecostal church. That was the family argument, church and more church.

Did I want this God to whom Fout was as important as Tessa?

60

Mark Cabot
Grace Cabot's Breakdown

"I think of Fout torturing those people—then coming into our church, *our church*, and sitting next to us, smearing us with his guilt." Grace was crying—spitting as she talked. She was not Grace. I had not seen this woman before.

"It is not our church," I said. "It is God's church. I'm as distraught as you. I have come to the bottom of myself. I have faced my own terror and anger and rage at this man. He has undone what has taken years of work." I tried to hold her, to calm her.

"No, no." She tried to push me back, but I held her.

"Grace—" I tried to reason with her.

"You're on his side. You go to see him all the time."

"I've only been a few times," I said, but I saw reason would not work. "You know the verse in Matt 25:36: 'When I was in prison you visited me.'"

"You bring murder into the house. I know you have to defend the church—but something has happened to me. Something has come between us. I can't let anyone else quiz me about Thomas Fout and why he was in our church and why we didn't know, and I think of his smearings over me and Clare—I think of his rope around us." Grace was crying again. She was hitting her head with her hands. What was wrong with her? I pulled her to the couch with all my might and held her down so she wouldn't throw herself into something. She was wild. Inconsolable. I felt Grace struggling, trying to get out from under me. She was stronger than I had known. It was taking all my strength to hold her there.

My face was right in front of Grace's—almost touching it—but not with a kiss. I shot words at her, as if it was myself to whom I was speaking, shouting, drilling the words into her.

So this is how couples felt who came to counseling sessions—this is what had gone on before they had come. This is how they had wounded one another. This was the secret they kept. They tried to tell without telling me. I obviously had not understood how they got close to one another and felt the hot breath of humanity, the boiler room. The bare closeness was frightening.

"Let me up."

"I can't, Grace. Not until you settle down."

"Settle down? Let them lick me with their eyes—the minister's wife who housed a murderer."

"Let them look at you."

"No," Grace was hysterical again. I'd said the wrong thing. I felt her body heaving, not so much pushing me off, but all of it: the murders, the murdered, the murderer. She struggled again, pushing against me with every bit of strength she had.

"Stop it, Grace. You're acting crazy. I can't let you up. You'll hurt yourself."

Grace continued to cry and at the same time speak. Her words did not make sense—she was speaking from within herself—almost to someone else—not to me. But who? Herself, yes, but also to God? To the idea of justice itself?

Did I need help with her? Who could I call? Who could help me hold her? Roy? The doctor? I wanted to call a minister, but I was the minister. I couldn't separate myself from myself and become two. I wished we had family in Buckholt. I continued to hold her. She seemed to tire. The thrusts of her body against me were not as strong. Was this what Thomas Fout had experienced? The force of a body against his? The exhilaration? No, it was not exhilaration. It made me uneasy. We had been married fifteen years, and I had not felt her in this way. It was a transgression of our relationship—an invasion of her space. I was where I was not wanted.

"I can't stand this." Grace seemed calmer. "He brought murder into our church. You have worked so hard to establish a congregation and he soured it, smeared it with his wickedness. I can't even think of the word—"

Mark Cabot: Grace Cabot's Breakdown

"'Evil' is the word you want. We've seen it. It has been with us."

Grace covered her ears as I spoke. I thought she would remain quiet, but she became agitated again. I had not known she was capable of such distress. She shuffled her feet quickly in place. I could hardly believe it was Grace in the room with me.

Why did I remember the tiny noise of the snake by the dock at Orbson Lake? The squeak—no, the scream?

Grace was coming apart. I went to grab her. She struggled away.

"Grace—Grace—" I tried to reach her with my voice, my familiarity, my assurance. Though she resisted, I held her. She was trembling violently now.

"I can't do this. I can't stay here. I am going back to my mother's. I called her. I have to wait for Clare to get out of school."

"You didn't tell me?" I said. "You can't run."

"I'm not staying!" she screamed.

"We can't run from it," I told her.

"You can't hold me here."

I continued to hold her down. She seemed to rest a moment. She seemed almost rational.

"Let me get my cell phone out of my pocket. I'll call the doctor. He can give you something to help." With that, she became hysterical again. She did not want to be drugged. She did not want medicine. She wanted to be as far away as possible from this place. How could she let Clare breathe another moment of this air? This evil place. Why couldn't I see what hell it was? What *hell*! Grace screamed.

I was frightened. Who was this strange woman, crazy with—what? Anxiety? That was my guess. I had seen it before in counseling. But never this close. Never breathing under me. She was like a large bird I held down. Her hair was across my face. I could feel the heat of her breath beneath it.

Had I brought my cell phone from the office? Sometimes I forgot it there. I let go of Grace's arm and felt my pocket. The phone was there.

Grace was flailing with her arm loose in the air, and I grabbed her arm again and held it over her head. Maybe a neighbor would come over to see what the disruption was—this ruckus at the quiet minister's house. Maybe they would think someone was in trouble and would come to help. What time was it? How soon would Clare be home? Did she have something after school? Was Grace supposed to pick her up? I held her once again against another outburst. Then I let go of her arm once more and reached for the cell phone in the pocket of my trousers. Grace nearly pushed me to the floor with her weight. I had to balance myself with one foot on the floor to hold her on the couch. I held both of her arms with one hand and tried to open the phone and dial with the other. It wasn't going to work. It took both hands to hold her down. Both arms. My whole body.

"Grace," I spoke when she was silent and out of breath, "you've got to come back to yourself. In the name of Jesus—think about this—you're a rational woman. This is not you. Listen," I spoke quietly against her ear, "you have come apart. You'll need some help in getting back. You can go to your mother's with Clare. I'll drive you there. I'll stay with you if—" She struggled again and I broke off my thought. "Shhhhh, shhhhhh," I quieted her. In another moment, I got my cell phone open and called 911.

Grace was admitted to the hospital. She slept there overnight and was released the next morning, shaken and pale. I called her brother in McPherson. He and his wife came for her. They were used to emergencies. They were used to human frailty. I asked if I could come with her to see her family in McPherson. Grace did not want me.

Clare looked from the back window as they drove off.

61

Grace Cabot
McPherson

When I got home, I went to the cemetery where we had buried Tessa Margaret Cabot. I stood facing the wind from the southwest. I felt as shaky as the cemetery pines. How often the Kansas wind seemed strong enough to blow me away. I remembered when, as a child, the books in my satchel seemed to be the only things holding me down as I walked home from school.

The days with my family in McPherson, Kansas, were black. I wished I hadn't brought Clare, but she had her cousins to play with. My sisters-in-law made sure she was taken care of. They kept her away from me when I was despondent. If we stayed long enough, Clare would go to school. But for now, she had her study packet.

Who was this God who had given me only two children, then took one back? I felt betrayed. Abandoned. Played with. Made fun of. Stripped. Raped. Tortured. Killed. Who was this God? A machine that ran the world? The thought of no God occurred to me, but I dismissed it. I'd been too long with ministers. I knew that God was. My brother reminded me this wasn't a crisis of belief—of faith. It was a crisis of mistrust. No, I could murder my thought of God. Let him exist on his own. Let him fill heaven with people who could take whatever he gave out.

He was a God who was there, but I had to hide from him.

I remembered passages in the Bible I'd always hated. Women received their dead raised to life again. Others were tortured, not accepting deliverance, that they might obtain a better resurrection. And others had trials of cruel mockings and scourgings, bonds and imprisonment. They were stoned, were sawn asunder, were tested, were slain with the sword; they wandered in sheepskins and goatskins, destitute, afflicted, tormented (of whom the world was not worthy). They wandered in deserts, in mountains, and in dens and caves of the earth. They received not the promise, God having provided some better thing.[1]

I had been in church all my life, but I had not known. I cried as I had not cried before. Great sobs shook my body. I could not stop sobbing. I sobbed and sobbed until I feared I was coming apart again, this time for good. It wasn't fair. Women had received their dead raised to life again. I would have received Tessa back, but I did not have the choice. I would have accepted deliverance, but it was not offered.

"There's another part of that Scripture," Edward, my oldest brother offered, now in the room with me, "it comes before that passage: 'Who, through faith, subdued kingdoms, stopped the mouths of lions, quenched the violence of fire, escaped the edge of the sword, out of weakness were made strong.'"[2]

A better resurrection. There were resurrections and better resurrections? Lesser and greater?

1. Heb 11:35–39.
2. Heb 11:33.

62

Zelda Gheary
Now the Drawings Have Voices

I heard voices with my *subworld* drawings as I worked in the second bedroom. They weren't loud. They weren't anything I heard with my ears. But they were there somewhere inside my head. One day I drew Jesus on my sketchpad. He had a sour look on his face: Were you bored on your father's farm? So you packed your camel and started across the sky. You came to the corral of earth that holds us prisoners. You left your camel outside camp to wait your return from the cross. You had to forget heaven to live here on earth, but with Scripture, some of your mission came back. You had your twelve companions, one of them a dud, to do some fishing, to make a speech. To talk in parables so no one would understand. To handle it yourself. To hold their lives in your hands. In band, you played the cello. The miserable, lonely sound. No one wanted to listen to a man walking on the water, or even land, with a camel waiting outside the wall. It was too slow. Too dull.

    I drew the face of Jesus high on the wall in a far corner of the small room. It was a small face. I could hardly see it from the door of the room.

63

Mark Cabot
Separation

Thomas Fout had separated us—a minister and his wife. Should I tell Thomas that Grace had left me? But had she really left me? No, she had left the situation. No, I didn't want to give Thomas any personal information. I did not want to share. Thomas had worked his way between Grace and me. He had caused me personal grief, as well as fundamental, doctrinal grief. Could a murderer get into heaven? If Judas had called out to God the moment before he hanged himself, would he have entered heaven? Yes? No? Maybe? This blurring of boundaries—these questions Thomas opened up.

But there were many questions, many doubtings of the gospel. It had been that way from the beginning. And when they were assembled with the elders and had taken counsel, they gave large money to the soldiers, telling them to say his disciples came by night and stole him away while we slept.[1]

Now there were many books refuting the gospel or casting doubt—just blurring it a little, changing it just enough to remove the sting—or simply questioning, could this really be true?

There was even a new book saying that Judas was called aside by Jesus to be the beloved one—to be initiated into some sort of secret wisdom—to

---

1. Matt 28:12–13.

Mark Cabot: Separation

be more than the traitor he was in the gospels. How foolish. How many more things would attempt to shake faith? Even the elect would be confused.[2]

There had always been confusion. Is Christ divided? Was Paul crucified for you?[3]

We prayed for the evil in the world—that it would be contained. We prayed for the Taliban and Al Qaeda, for jihad and militant Muslims. We asked that our prayers would stump the plans of the terrorists or turn them back or hinder them in some way. We prayed for the protection and security of our nation. We had prayed for the war in Iraq, and for America's commitments abroad. We prayed for the church families that had sons and daughters in the armed services, for the men and women in the military. We spoke peace to the sleep of the soldiers. We spoke confusion to the insurgents. We prayed for the evil in our own lives. We prayed for the power to withstand it. The men's prayer group met once a week on Thursday mornings beginning at 6:30, some men coming earlier or later depending on their work, or someone in trouble stopping by for prayer, but usually there were eight or nine who gathered in the sanctuary of the church. Gheary, Saith, Weldon, Stanton, Keller, Ramos, Furnish, Wilkens, and the new president of the congregation, Kester. The deacons. We prayed for the economic strain on families, for oil prices, heating and gasoline, for the direction of us all toward the unknown. We prayed for migrant workers who came from Mexico. Sometimes they were hurt on their construction or roofing jobs and were away from their families. Men from the prayer group would visit them, help return them to Mexico for rehabilitation, or bring their families here. But this particular morning, we sat quietly in the sanctuary of the church. I was the pastor; I was supposed to know what to say.

We were past the shock. But now there were the aftershocks.

I testify of the world—that its works are evil.[4]

I was trying to bring us through the crisis, but I began to see how far *through* would be. In fact, I couldn't see the end. I had underestimated it. I wondered if it would ever be over.

2. Mark 13:22.
3. 1 Cor 1:13.
4. John 7:7.

At night, I felt like Samuel when he was called up from the dead, disgruntled, to answer a question from Saul.[5]

I felt my anger all over again, just when I thought I had it under control. I realized Grace was another victim of Fout.

What made my congregation put in the effort to come to church on Sunday mornings? To get breakfast, to get the children dressed, to get past the balking, the crying, the uphill pull, only to be faced with a sermon and a collection plate? I also held Sunday night services and Wednesday evening services. There were other meetings: the board of deacons, prayer groups, Bible studies. What made them tithe? Give up their money they could otherwise use.

In turn, I was supposed to prop them up. Give them sermons, those war manuals. Instruct them in the art of spiritual warfare. I was there to tell them we had gathered to praise God because of his mercy upon us. Because at the end of it all there was something called eternal life, and it made a difference in how we lived our lives. No, good behavior was not how we got into heaven. It was faith in Jesus Christ. A public declaration of him. The people could reject the idea of eternal life. They could even reject the idea of God. But it was a gamble I would not want to take.

"Why do you come to church?" I asked Roy Saith.

"I've come all my life. My parents brought me. I need God. Christ is fundamental to who I am."

"You don't seem to have needs that would drive you here."

"There's a hunger beyond material satisfaction," Roy said. "Surely you know that."

---

5. 1 Sam 28:12.

64

Zelda Gheary
Covered Dishes

Mark kept the church suppers going in Grace's absence. The women continued to bring their covered dishes. I took the women's meetings while Grace was gone. I think Mark wanted Beth Saith to take them, but Ralph argued for me. I let the other women pray and take the lessons. Then I went back to my workroom and continued the small circles that traveled across the ceiling.

We were driven like sheep into a pen that was not static but was moving inward, getting smaller, more cramped all the time. Were we the covered dishes? Were we to know what it was to be sacrificed like animals? I looked at a postcard I had bought at the Kimbell Art Museum in Fort Worth, Carracci's *The Butcher's Shop*. I drew the carcass of animals. I drew ourselves split open, trussed up. I felt sick inside as I drew. I drew the sickness on the ceiling above me. I called the whole room *The Butcher's Shop*. All the disappointed people Ralph and Mark counseled were there. All the sad frames in which their lives hung. No, *our* lives. I was one of them. Implicated by the act of being in Buckholt. The innards we all knew were there. We felt and tasted. I drew them smaller and smaller all the time. I drew *us* smaller and smaller. All the smattering. All the hurt. All the weight of those covered dishes in our hands. All the distress living at the bone.

65

Grace Cabot
Tessa

McPherson, Kansas, was my refuge. I had gone to Trinity Lutheran Church. I knew where Maxwell Road turned into gravel. I knew the names of the streets: Mallard, Hickory, Chestnut, Cherry, Hawthorne. I knew the Opera House at Main and Sutherland. The McPherson Museum on Euclid. Kansas Avenue that also was Highway 56. The two-story brick house on Euclid near the museum where my parents lived. The fall leaves that turned red. Central Christian College and McPherson College. There were still a few old brick streets. The newer houses were north of First Street. The large Catholic and Covenant churches stood on Northwest Avenue.

I knew the cemetery. The milo field beyond the cemetery. The small flat stone near the trees on the north. There was no lamb on Tessa's grave, as there were on the infants' graves. Tessa was too old. A flat stone etched with her name and a Bible verse. Mark had wanted a verse adapted from *The Brothers Karamazov*: "She is with the angels singing before God." No, no, I told him. We had fought. I was not going to have it. Why did Mark like that book? In the end, we decided on "Of such is the kingdom of God."[1] Now I stood before the stone. Of such is the kingdom. Would that be dead children? Maybe I should have listened to Mark. Was the destination of my life in briers, thorns, and bramble?

---

1. Luke 18:16.

Grace Cabot: Tessa

I had kept my Bible in a cloth cover with lace around the edges. The Bible had represented order. Simplicity. Now it tore me open. It had not protected. I took my Bible out of its cover and stared at the hard, black cover.

I had left my husband because he had the ball in his hands. He had the dangerous job. I couldn't stand it yet. Who were the secret people? The man with the jar of water that led the apostles to the last supper.[2] How many were in on it? This conspiracy of God against me.

I enrolled Clare in school. I stayed in McPherson the rest of the school year.

When Bible school approached at the beginning of summer, I called Mark and told him I couldn't help.

"I've already got help," he said. "I don't think there will be many children—other than the usual members. We won't be sending the bus around. I don't think parents would let their children come. Maybe next year . . ." Mark paused. I heard him sigh. I knew his thought. We might never recover. It was the same sigh I heard in the rectory after Tessa died. And he was right. We might never recover.

"How have you been?"

"I'm taking medication. Clare's aunts and cousins are taking care of her. I have time to myself to get depressed. Clare has asked to come back. You can come for her if you want. She's always liked Bible school."

"I'm going to leave her there with you," Mark said. "I've needed this time."

"You'd think we would need to be together," I said.

"It tore us apart in different ways—we had to separate to face this part of it."

"My brother has helped me."

"If Clare asks again, I'll come and get her," Mark told me. "I hope we'll be back together soon."

"Has Ben's new wife had her nose in Bible school?"

"She's actually been a help."

There was a strange sense of release I felt. I was free of the hassle of vacation Bible school. Hassle? When had I thought in those terms before? Vacation Bible school was a chance for children who had never heard it to

---

2. Luke 22:10.

hear the name of Jesus. I would have to get a hold of myself. Mark had told me I was not myself. I remembered his strength as he held me down.

If I was a stranger to myself, he was a stranger to me also. He had seen my weakness. I felt as vulnerable and exposed to him as I did to the public. I was embarrassed. Our relationship had changed. It had changed in a way I could not yet determine. All I knew was that I felt a hard place inside myself.

I sat at supper with Clare. Just the two of us went to a restaurant. No family. Just us.

"Are you ready to go home?" I asked.

"When you are. Dad said he would come and get us anytime."

"When did you talk to him?"

"He calls on Aunt Ellie's phone," Clare said. "He knows I'm with her."

"I'm sorry I haven't been available." How stupid that sounded to me.

"I know you've been upset."

When had Clare begun to speak as a adult?

"Yes, I have," I answered.

I watched Clare eat her hamburger. She didn't seem worried over the separation from her father or her mother. She seemed grounded. She was all right.

66

Mark Cabot
I Woke Trembling One Morning

I felt something step back into the darkness as I woke. Maybe it was hope that anything would be normal again. I planned to visit Thomas Fout that afternoon. I felt my depression. But I believed that everything had a purpose. After this separation from Grace, maybe I could better understand what others felt.

I also had Ralph Gheary to worry about. His reaction was like Roy Saith's. I was afraid they would become vigilantes and ride to the prison at Wyatt and kill Thomas Fout. But Gheary was in the ministry. He wanted to be a minister. He had been ordained in the seminary. I could request that he be transferred to another church, but I didn't want that stain on his record. I was a minister also. I had to consider him. Zelda Gheary also was unpredictable. I liked her, and I think Grace liked her also, though many of the wives did not. She was lively, exuberant at times. I felt she was what the church needed for its dreariness. But I saw in her the same flash of anger I saw in Ralph. Could they be trusted as shepherds through this valley?

Thomas Fout had brought the body of one of his victims into Christ Church. What was there about that that did not induce rage? I wondered if the church could be haunted by that act—if it were horrific enough that demons attended and remained after the body was removed. I put that thought out of my mind. Christ had charge over his church. Had he not driven those from the church he did not want in the church? Thomas had killed over his lunch hour. It marked him as a sociopath. Thomas Fout had a tree house behind his home where his children had played. After they were grown, he reviewed the souvenirs of his murders there, going over them in his mind. Or did he hide them while his children played there still? Fout was going to make an impact. What kept Ruth Fout from knowing? Was I angry with her too?

After the sop, Satan, entered him.[1] Maybe Satan entered Thomas Fout as he had Judas. Where were these openings that Satan could enter? It was a decision to do evil. A loss of judgment. He was the snake under the ramp. I had to remind myself that I had put my shovel on its neck.

I was aware of my depression because of the inertia I felt. To make matters worse, I listened to a book on tape on my trip to Wyatt—Jakob Walter's *The Diary of a Napoleonic Foot Soldier*. In June 1812, six hundred thousand men crossed into Russia. In December 1812, only twenty-five thousand had survived to re-cross the border. Life had always been horrific. I felt like I was tramping through a frozen field in Russia with Jakob. From time to time, the church had sent Bibles and other support to underground churches in Russia. We had asked ourselves what kind of faith we could maintain if we could be persecuted for it.

"Some people don't think I am a Christian, but I think I am."

"You brought a dead body into the church," I said to Fout at Wyatt Prison. "You are a Christian murderer. How does one understand that?"

Fout looked at me without answering.

"The fearful, and unbelieving, and the abominable, and murderers," I quoted from Rev 21:8, "have their part in the lake that burns with fire and brimstone, which is the second death."

There was evil in heaven. It would be thrown out at the final judgment. God let it go for the time being. He put up with it. So could I.

"It is possible to know and feel, but not act upon it." I began what seemed like a sermon to Tom, "To feel oneself respond to something one should not respond to. To feel yourself respond, yet abstain."

Fout was bitter about his wife.

"She had to divorce you," I said. "She couldn't be connected to what you have done. She couldn't separate you from your actions."

"Can you?"

"I don't know," I said.

1. John 13:27.

"The ruts became too deep to get out of," Fout said. "I kept killing. I felt possessed."

"The first time I killed there was an exhilaration. I felt a sense of completion. I had played with the idea a long time. I had toyed. Then I acted upon it."

Were demons a possibility? Ralph had first suggested it. Yes, maybe that was it. That was the way out. It wasn't Fout but demons that were at fault.

"One of the wives said as I started to strangle her, 'God have mercy on your soul.'"

"What made you continue?"

"I was prepared. I had planned. I had my murder kit: plastic bag, rope, tape, knife. I had nothing else to do—my work at the time wasn't interesting. Maybe I was between jobs. I knew how to cut phone wires. I had installed security systems. I compartmentalized in my life. I separated victims from their families. I killed for relief of tension. I would rather do anything but this." Here Fout paused, "That's not true. I returned to it again and again. I would have gone back. The desire to do it again was coming. I felt an overwhelming urge to kill. I desired it. I wanted to feel the power of taking someone's life."

It took all my energy to listen to Fout. That night, I fell into bed. Sleep always renewed me, even without Grace beside me. But this sleep was troubled. The turmoil I felt would not let up. It followed me into the night. I thought about demon possession. I felt the damage Fout had done to the families of the victims. They would be marred for the rest of their lives. How would I recover to shepherd my flock? Would I recover?

People looked at me in the stores. Is this what Grace had felt? What I would give to have her back.

But Christianity had teeth. It could eat bones. It brought us to the hard core of ourselves that could not be with God without Christ's act of redemption on the cross.

67

Zelda Gheary
Soot

I heard barking as I drew that night. I made circles stirred by a fiery wind. A flaming tornado picked up a house and set it down on a green-faced witch. I worked on my *subworld* drawings. They would cover the walls of the second bedroom. I thought of placing a lock on the door of my workroom. What if Ralph discovered them again? What would he do if he saw the ceiling in my workroom? The enormity of them? The number of them? I had a tremendous thought: Prison was a place without paintings. I mean, that was Fout's punishment.

Ralph was still at the church when Dr. Edwards called. He had a possible position for Ralph in the pastorate—this one in another state.

"Ralph won't go," I told him. "I'd leave in a minute, but Thomas Fout has the cross nailed to the church."

There was a pause on the other end of the phone. "Nice talking to you, Zelda."

I went back to work in my *subworld*. Deeper and deeper in the soot. It was as if I was in a furnace. I had pencil smearings on my hands. My arms. The table where I worked. Papers on which I had not yet drawn. There seemed to be cinders in the air. Sometimes I coughed from them.

"I and my Father are one."[1] I worked with that thought. Thomas Fout had set himself up as God. He had made himself the decider of life and death. He chose his victims. He executed them.

1. John 10:30.

Zelda Gheary: Soot

Was it a decision we all were brought to? I was the god of my drawings. I decided which way the pencil went, which way the shadings marked the white wall. It was power I felt.

68

Mark Cabot
Mark Retrieves His Wife and Daughter

I decided to go to McPherson to retrieve my broken wife and bewildered daughter, if Grace would let me. Mildred said she would have the women who cleaned the church clean the parsonage also. Grace and I would come back to church as damaged people who stood at the cross for healing.

"Can you preach this Sunday without blasting the congregation out of their seats?" I asked Ralph Gheary, "I'm going to McPherson."

Ralph looked up from his desk to see if I was serious. He nodded his head.

"I worry about your fury," I said. "Can we pray before I leave?"

"I would choke on it."

"I won't," I said. "God, bless this man and his righteous indignation. He is right. He is right. He is right. But your ways are not our ways. Let him see from your way."

I was nothing without the Scripture. I had no wisdom. I was foolish. Satan had sat in my congregation and laughed. I was left at the end of my tolerance. I was without answers. What good was I? A minister should have the answers. Had I slept through seminary? Had I learned anything in my years of service? Of leadership? How I was brought to foolishness. Yet I confessed with my mouth that Satan would not have power over me. Since

Mark Cabot: Mark Retrieves His Wife and Daughter

Fout's arrest, I had received many calls, many letters, many cards containing much advice and suggestion—even the need for exorcism for the demon-possessed, which the writer of the letter felt was Fout's case. I considered them all, though the thought of demon possession continued to haunt me. But for now, I would get up again. I would drive to McPherson. Where were my keys? Where was my car? I left the house. I returned to the house to lock it. I looked in my pocket to make sure I had my wallet. I would have to buy gas. I would spend several hours driving to McPherson. I would think. I would have answers. I imagined what I would say.

They were sitting down to dinner when I entered my father-in-law's house. I couldn't say anything I had planned. Clare got up from her chair and came to put her arms around me. I broke before her and wept. Grace was at my side then too. We had been defeated. We had been shamed. We had to turn around and go back to the point of our hurt and shame. It was not easy to wipe off the dust—to walk when Thomas Fout had tripped us. We couldn't go on as though nothing happened. We couldn't act as though we weren't wounded. My in-laws surrounded us. They prayed for us as we wept, lifting us up in the light of Christ. Afterwards, I sat at the table with my in-laws. I listened to their words.

"Grace, we have a ministry," I said when I could talk. "We're going back to Buckholt to get on our knees and pray for strength. God will not let us perish. We are going to be a family. I need you there."

The next morning, we drove back to Buckholt. I had my wife and daughter. They were quiet. But they were there—as certain as those two men had been in my office in the beginning.

69

Ralph Gheary
His Sermon

"I begin with a verse I've heard Pastor Cabot use: 'There was a little city and a few men within it; and there came a great king against it, and besieged it, and built great bulwarks against it' (Eccl 9:14).

"There was a little city: Buckholt, Kansas. A great king came against it, and his name was Evil. What is evil? Where is it? I had thought of demon possession at first. Then I thought, it would be excusing Thomas Fout. It would be misplacing blame. Evil is an act of decision. It is a bud we carry in the ribcage, close to the heart. It is fenced. We can prevent it from blooming. We can stop its attempts to leave its enclosure—but we can't get rid of it.

"What happened to Thomas Fout? Why did he let Evil blossom and overgrow this little city? What made him enter a house during his lunch hour, murder, then return to work as if nothing had happened? What caused him to haul a body into church, then attend Sunday service knowing what he had done? We are small and stupid against Evil. Where was the part in seminary about stepping into the underlife? The underworld of a murderer? The murky world.

"Why has Evil bothered us on this magnitude? Are we worthy to fight such an enemy? Why didn't Evil go and bother someone larger? A nation, for instance, which in fact it has and does. But why Buckholt, Kansas? Evil seeps in where it can. A man named Thomas Fout had a little bud of Evil in him. He was born with it. He felt it. He watered it. He didn't cut back its tendrils with any judgment or thought of saying, 'I will not do this.' He dwelt on Evil. Made love to it. Harbored it. Let it loose on a family, killing his first victims—a father, mother, and two children. Yes, we have a murderer in our midst. Do they not err that devise Evil?[1] Does that mean they do wrong? Or in their wrong, will they make an error? Evil is something we bring from within. My dictionary calls it, 'up from under.' Do you think Evil is an abstract idea? Look at the bodies. Look at the broken blood vessels in the faces that were strangled, released to breathe again, then strangled again. Evil is with us. It is us.

"But where does Evil come from? Evil even passes through the mind of God, but he is not tempted.[2] Is it not there in the beginning of the Bible? The tree of the knowledge of Good and Evil is there in Gen 2:9. And Satan is there to tempt Adam and Eve, saying, 'Eat, you shall be as gods, knowing Good and Evil.' God had told them not to eat, but in an act of decision, an act of disobedience, they ate. And the Lord God said, 'The man is become as one of us, to know Good and Evil.'[3] Soon God saw that the imagination of the thoughts of the heart was only Evil continually.[4] The serpent was here to destroy.

"But where did Satan come from? Evil was pre-existing. It was there before us.

"Satan was an angel—one of the beings God created to be with him. Satan was the most beautiful. 'I am like God,' he thought. 'I am God. I will do what I want. I will take life where I can. I will cause suffering and loss. I will openly attack. I will be subtle. They won't feel my presence until it is too late. They will laugh when anyone mentions my name. I will not be taken seriously. I will be a joke. Meanwhile I strike—I gut—I take.'

"According to the Bible, God expelled Satan from Heaven with some of his friends. In the book of Job, we find Satan still sulking around God's throne. Satan always is plotting. He can get through the walls of a church and provoke its members. He can bring down towers. He can get through the smallest cracks. He can incite a nation. He can bring unspeakable destruction in the smallest place. It is the will. The pride of will driven by the ego.

"How you are fallen from heaven, O Lucifer, son of the morning. How you are cut down to the ground, you who did weaken the nations. For you

1. Prov 14:22.
2. Jas 1:13.
3. Gen 3:22.
4. Gen 6:5.

said in your heart, 'I *will* ascend into heaven; I *will* exalt my throne above the stars of God; I *will* sit also upon the mount of the congregation, in the sides of the north; I *will* ascend above the heights of the clouds. I *will* be like the Most High.' And they will look upon you narrowly and say, 'Is this the man who made the earth tremble and who did shake kingdoms, who made the world like a wilderness and destroyed its cities, who opened not the house of his prisoners?'[5]

"Do you not think families are destroyed by Satan? By the evil he stirs up. It is already there within us. This is horrific news. This is the news that is ignored. Where is the brotherhood of man when Thomas Fout, with his full garden in bloom, looks in a window?"

Ruth Fout was in the choir. From the corner of my eye, I saw her stand and leave through the choir door. One of the women left with her. In a moment, I thought of her fleeing the church, back through the shock of Tom's arrest, back farther through their quiet marriage—the first days of their marriage, the simple wedding, their engagement, her job, the hope of marriage, school, her girlhood—the way someone's life passes before them in an instant. I was sidetracked momentarily, but I returned to my sermon.

"I am plowed under by the arrest of Thomas Fout. I feel at times I am helpless against it. Wisdom is better than weapons of war, but one sinner destroys much good.[6] O God, remove me from the overgrowth of Evil. Take it from my house. Remove it from the downspouts. I cannot find forgiveness. When I think of him—if he got into my house when I wasn't there, if he had harmed Zelda . . . I have been crazy with that thought. At times, my imagination will not quit. I could murder him with my own hands. I would have. I know it. I was doing it in my thoughts. Nero. Hitler. Stalin. Mussolini. Idi Amin. Pol Pot. Saddam Hussein. It was just the beginning.

"What is this bloom I hear? I could murder Fout myself for smearing the church. It is the will, knocking to get out."

---

5. Isa 14:12–17.
6. Eccl 9:18.

70

Mark Cabot
Trouble Within

A flood of calls waited when I returned from McPherson. Why did I leave that weekend and ask Ralph Gheary to preach? I could have gone mid-week to retrieve my family, but there were times I had to be gone. I couldn't be in the pulpit every Sunday. Ralph had preached before. He always had been edgy. I liked that. It was the zeal I felt I had lost, and therefore, that the church had lost. He brought us back to the point. But the point he preached on Sunday may have been too sharp. I wondered again if I should let him go. It had been too much for him. It had been too much for me. It wouldn't be a dishonor. It wouldn't be a blot on his record.

Grace and I met with Ruth to apologize and to encourage her to return to church.

I listened to the complaints. Ralph had not recorded his message. Something had been wrong with the machine. The only one arguing for him was Roy Saith.

"He got to the point. He reached evil. It is nothing I wanted to hear, but I recognized the truth of it."

"Maybe we can't deal with truth."

"That's what I come to church for, pastor," Roy said to me. "If it was what I hear all week, I wouldn't show up."

"But there are shades of adjustable truth. Too much truth destroys. Upsets."

"I think it's your job to deal with truth."

One of Us

A few others called, one or two, probably prompted by Roy, to say they appreciated Ralph's stand against Fout.

I talked to Ralph Gheary about his sermon—how it had upset some of the congregation. He was as weary of the upheaval as I was.

71

Ralph Gheary
A Call

I called Dr. Edwards and told him I had been taken to task. I had preached what I felt was God's word to preach. Edwards gave me the usual exhortations. I was in a difficult situation. There would be backlash when I preached God's word, yet I should prayerfully consider the text of my message within the context of audience and situation.

We had talked over the months following the arrest of Thomas Fout. I confided in my seminary advisor more than in Mark Cabot. Cabot didn't question it, but I imagined he wondered, or hoped he wondered.

We continued to e-mail. I asked Edwards to look for another position for me. I felt Mark Cabot's disdain of me and my work.

"But think of the pressure he is under," Dr. Edwards said. "You may be in the place God wishes you to be."

Howard Edwards asked about Zelda, and I reassured him. She had upset the women's prayer group with her zealous voice, but I didn't go into it.

72

Mark Cabot
Exorcism

I wrote a letter to a church in Minnesota that had written me about exorcism.

Exorcism. That was it. Judas took the sop and the devil entered him. The spirit of wickedness walked in the world to find who it could enter. The spirits of wickedness. Those dark inclinations in the human heart. Those additions that led to developments in the human will. Evil urges, dark thoughts. Those ruts, those presences that attended thought, that were gotten used to, that were acted upon if we didn't guard against them, becoming one of us.

We were fishing in unclear water. Murky, unclean, and frightful.

Jesus had chosen fisherman to walk with him. Full of frailty and ignorance. What mystery we walked in. How could a fisherman have written, "In the beginning was the Word, and the Word was with God, and the Word was God"[1]?

I read the book of Mark, the oldest of the gospels, about casting out demons.

I flew to Minnesota to a church where they practiced exorcism.

I felt strange. I wasn't sure I should be going, but evil persuaded me to go. On the plane, I read *The Confessions of Saint Augustine*, book 7, chapter 3, "Free Will and the Problem of Evil"—or I tried to read. I had trouble

---

1. John 1:1.

concentrating. "Up to this time, although I affirmed and firmly believed . . . you, our Lord . . . I still had no . . . orderly knowledge of the cause of evil." I continued to read, though I couldn't follow what I read. Once in a while I connected to Saint Augustine's text. Was it our free will that was the cause of evil? Or an outside source? Where did that source come from, if not God, who created all things? I looked out the plane window again at the orderly fields below. I would have to return to the reading later, going back over and over it until I understood. I was too preoccupied, I tried to excuse myself. When I was bored with the land under the plane, I returned to the book. I reread the passage again. If evil came from Satan, where did he get it? The answer seemed to return to the free will the creator had given his creation. It wasn't what I wanted to read. I put the book down and resolved to watch the ground. There was a woman in the seat beside me. I was glad she didn't want to talk.

In Minnesota, I took a cab to the church. The cab driver was Muslim. I wanted to ask what his religion did with evil. I suppose the evil-doer was beheaded. How ignorant I was of other religions—of the world in general. How ignorant I was of my own religion's God.

At the church, I met with ministers and a few other people. I watched a documentary. I listened to the testimonies. I heard the details. I attended a rite of exorcism. I heard the coughings. The gagings. I felt a terrible fear. I felt as though a demon moved with me. I sweated. I shook. They comforted me with words of Scripture. They prayed. They said others felt the way I did in the presence of the confrontation of a demon. I saw the eventual release of evil. The departure. I had to sit in a chair. They prayed for my recovery. I felt as drained as the one who had been freed of his demon. I'm not sure I was convinced, but I felt that Fout could be possessed by a demon. I felt that he was. That was my conclusion.

I asked for an exorcism the next time I visited Wyatt. I would bring elders from the church with me. The prison refused. I think I was relieved. Maybe it was not my job to enter the horror of demon possession, just to know it was there.

That night as the plane lifted above Minneapolis and Saint Paul, I saw the lights of the cities. The blocks were in a grid—it reminded me of the inside of a computer.

I was still shaken by my experience. I sat in my office one morning and made a list of duties, of the tangible and practical ways I moved in the world.

My list included: Sunday services at Christ Church in Buckholt, church council meetings, district meetings of ministers, meetings with the bishop, church suppers the third Wednesday evening of every month, marriages (though there had not been many—the daughter of a member of the congregation was married in another church, which I understood), counseling sessions, hospital visits, funerals, the men's prayer group, interfaith council and ecumenical meetings (for which I had less tolerance as time went on), Clare's recitals and programs at school, visits to Grace's family in McPherson, to Edward and Philip, and their family's visits to us. But my roles of father and husband weren't duties. They were part of my fabric. My life.

I listed the families I could count on, Roy and Beth Saith, Molly and Sam Stanton, Jack Kester and his wife (What was her name?), Harriet and George Weldon, Edna Fraiser and the reliable churchwomen. Ben with his new wife (Ben should have married Edna). I even listed Ruth Fout because she still attended Christ Church.

I listed things I wanted to do, such as plant rhododendrons.

I did not list things of which I was certain, as I would have in the past.

I concentrated that morning on the normal. The mundane. The ordinary. Until it stopped me. It was a list of church duties that brought Thomas Fout down. It was his list of church duties that led authorities to him.

73

Ralph Gheary
The Unpardonable Sin

While Pastor Cabot was off learning about demons, I went to visit Thomas Fout at Wyatt. I had discarded my belief in demons. I knew they were there in the Bible. Possibly in countries without a Christian base. I knew it more than before. But I thought it was an easy out for Fout. It would remove blame. But evil was indwelt. I thought Thomas Fout was a marked man. I thought he would get what he gave. At times, I thought Fout himself was a demon. By that, I meant a man who had let evil mark him. Fout would stand before the judgment seat of God. He would stand before his victims. It would not be any more pleasant than when he faced their families in court.

"I remember thinking it was wrong and deciding to do it anyway," Fout told me. "I remember the division. I remember parting from the thought, 'Don't do it.' I never lost that thought, but it became weaker every time I stalked my next victim. It was a small echo. A voice from someone calling nearly out of earshot. I was going to kill again, and possibly again. But I had that thought every time I murdered. Dogging me."

"Do you think you're going to heaven?"

"Yes."

"Why?"

"I'm a Christian. Christians go to heaven."

"But you committed unpardonable acts. You broke the law. You're in jail."

One of Us

"Unbelief is the unpardonable sin. Not murder."

"I think it is less a demon and more a moral decision against the conscience. I think you purposefully decided to do every nasty act you could conceive of. I don't think you considered God at all. What dilemma you have brought to the Christian community. Did you think of it? Did you think of what you would do?"

I waited for Fout's answer, but I saw he was no longer interested in talking to me, and I left.

I had an e-mail when I returned to the church:

> Ralph, I was afraid we would have more children than we could handle and they would grow up feeling neglected. I was afraid we would have a child who would die of some terrible illness. I was afraid we'd grow distant from one another until we hardly knew who the other was. I was afraid of the distance I felt in some of the couples at church.

—Zelda

I e-mailed her back:

> Zelda, I was afraid I would not interpret God correctly. I was afraid I'd fail him. I was afraid I'd make some mistake from which I could not recover. I was afraid I'd find myself imperfect. I'm overzealous. I want a perfect ministry. Well, already that is not going to happen. I messed up at the starting gate.

—Ralph

Zelda and I began meeting together for prayer. We had prayed before our marriage. Afterwards, we had been busy with the move and getting settled. We met occasionally, but often let it go.

We shared troubling passages of Scripture. "The gifts and calling of God are without repentance."[1] Did that mean that Thomas Fout, if he was a Christian when he murdered, was still a Christian?

"Once we enter God's kingdom by faith—no matter what we do—we're still God's child? Nothing we do can remove us from the kingdom? Could that be true? How could that possibly be true?"

1. Rom 11:29.

Ralph Gheary: The Unpardonable Sin

I didn't have answers for Zelda's questions. Or at least not answers I would share with her. I felt more and more that Fout was doomed. He was guilty of murder. Not only of the victims, but their families, some of them marked with grief for life. God was a loving God, but he was a just God also. I could not find leniency toward Thomas Fout. I only judged him more.

74

Zelda Gheary
The Installation

This mess. This mess the church was in. This mess that was the church. It spilled into my work. It spilled into our house. We heard from the grieving. The mourners. The overburdened. The overlooked. When Ralph made his hospital calls, Thomas Fout was in the conversation. When Ralph counseled a boy bullied in school, the boy said they bullied him about his church. When Ralph counseled another boy angered at the strictness of his parents, the boy said he used Thomas Fout as an argument against church. When Ralph tried to counsel me, I didn't want to be counseled. I wanted to be transported into art again and again. I wanted to follow the associations—how I went from one drawing on the wall to the next. It would not be in the physical world, but in the ideas inside my head. These drawings were only a subtext to the construction I carried within. I thought of an installation—Paul Gauguin's *The Yellow Christ* hanging in the front of the church, with the stayers at Christ's feet and the goers climbing a far wall. I thought of the painting enlarged to the size of the church, with some of my *subworld* drawings in long trails around it. It was my work—the job I wanted. My installation would never be allowed by Christ Church or by my husband. But it was my mission, my dream. Would Christ have come to the exhibit? Yes. It was about him.

75

Mark Cabot
There Were Other Murders in Kansas

Grace, Clare, and I ate in Aunt Mae's restaurant with the Saiths. People looked at us. I heard stress in Grace's voice as we ordered. Clare sat with the three Saith children at a large, round table near ours.

There was the Clutter family in Holcolm. The Andrews murders in Wolcott. Lowell Lee Andrews had confessed to his minister in the Grandview Baptist Church in Kansas City, Kansas, that he killed his parents and sister. There were others. I couldn't remember the names. They were on death row. Possibly in Leavenworth. They were outsiders to the church. But a member of my congregation at Wyatt?

"Let's not talk about Fout anymore," Grace said. "I'm tired of perversion."

I felt my depression as I ate. I could wrap my hands around Tom's throat, strangle him until he was dead. I think I felt hated for him. It was all because of him. I should be on death row because of what I was thinking.

I realized I was lost in thought. Had Roy asked a question? Grace and Beth were looking at me. I had to fight my way out of my thoughts. I had to talk to Roy, Beth, and Grace.

I looked the children at the round table. There were five chairs. One was vacant. I looked at Grace, who looked at me. Yes, I saw the empty chair that would have been Tessa's.

One of Us

There was a war in heaven. Michael and his angels fought against the dragon, and the dragon fought against his angels, and they could not prevail. Neither was their place found anymore in heaven. And the great dragon was cast out, that old serpent called the devil and Satan, who deceived the whole world. He was cast out into the earth, and his angels were cast out with him.[1]

Yes, the serpent had gone to live on earth. Hadn't I found one under the ramp that went into Orbson Lake? But there were others. They were everywhere. I had killed a snake there once, but the enemy was always there, accusing, causing torment. But I had power. I said it out loud to myself in my office.

I continued reading in Revelation. And I heard a loud voice saying in heaven, "Now is come salvation, and strength, and the kingdom of our God, and the power of his Christ; for the accuser of our brothers is cast down, who accused them before our God night and day. And they overcame him by the blood of the Lamb, and by the word of their testimony."[2]

There it was. My weapon. The blood of the Lamb. The word of my mouth. I testify to the power of God Almighty. The enemy came like a flood. The enemy caused havoc in the church. But we overcame by the shed blood of Christ and by the power of our testimony.

I was in the pit. Yet Christ reigns and would lift me up again. It was his power, not mine. The murder of murder. The murder of sin in the holy land that looked so much like Kansas.

I visited Fout in the state prison in Wyatt. I could hardly stay away from him. I was possessed. It's what Grace said, "You're possessed with him." I think I was. I had to get at the core of this. The seat of the problem. He was getting the better of me. Fout was in prison. Justifying himself. It wasn't his fault if it were demons.

"How did they come into you?"

"I remember as a child entertaining thoughts that were—I don't know how to describe it."

"Try."

"It's not normal, I suppose. I had sexual thoughts."

"I think we all do."

1. Rev 12:7–9.
2. Rev 12:11.

"It was more than thinking. I would get aroused even as a boy. It had to do with pain. With punishment."

"Where did these thoughts come from?"

"I don't know. They were there. I had no way to get rid of them. I knew they were wrong. That's why I didn't tell anyone. I knew I would be in trouble. It was my own possession—these thoughts—these arousals. It was exciting. It was a secret power. It was the place I wanted to be. The thoughts just kept going, growing as I got older. I would feel high. I would feel like someone other than myself. When I walked into the house the first time I killed—I walked into a house not mine. There were people there. Children. I spoke with authority. I tied them up. They complied. It was a thrill. I was sacred. I was exhilarated. There was nothing like it. There's never been anything like it. I would try not to think about it. I tried to suppress it. To stop it."

"You told the newspaper you knew who your next victim was."

"Yes, I had been scouting it out for a while. Maybe a year or more. Maybe years. It seemed like it was over—being in church—my job as compliance officer. Some of the power was there. But not enough, finally. I would have killed again."

"Who would you have killed?"

"A woman I'd been watching. It doesn't matter."

"It matters to her. To us. To God."

"It was no one in church. No one you would know."

"The demon returned?"

"The demon never left. I was just able to handle it for a while."

"How did you live with the guilt?"

"I didn't feel a lot of guilt. I felt sorry I had to live without the excitement I had known."

"How did you listen to my sermons? How did you sing?"

"That part of me is still here too."

I fell asleep late that night. I thought of our conversation. I didn't want to share with Grace. The less she knew, the better. I didn't want her tainted anymore than she already was. I didn't want to smear her with the unclean. I didn't want her to leave me again.

I felt my dreams that night almost before I was asleep. I would not drive to the state prison at Wyatt so often. It took nearly the whole day to drive there, visit with him, and return to Buckholt. Then I had to stop by the office and read my messages. My sermon notes floated in the air. They spoke in the wind. Then there was a dark cloud. The tail of a tornado came from the sky. I saw it was a knife. I saw it was a rope. There was Thomas Fout. I saw the image of his face before me. He came in the tornado? As the tornado? Behind the tornado? He was the tornado. It was hard to tell. Dreams were jumbled. The power I felt was fear. It gripped my neck. It shut off my air. I was strangling in the tail of the tornado. A hand was on my arm.

"Mark! Mark—wake up, you're dreaming." It was Grace. For a moment, Fout didn't go away. I was afraid he was actually in the room. Grace was in danger. I leapt from the bed. I had to protect her. "Mark!" She turned on the light. I struggled to leave the dream, shielding my eyes against the brightness. I stood by the bed in a sweat. Terrified.

Soon we heard Clare's footsteps. Had I woken her? What kind of noise had I made in my dream? Clare got into bed with us. We held her between us, trembling from the intrusion of Thomas Fout.

A few nights later, I woke from another dream. I think I was stalking someone. A man was ahead of me. I had been waiting to follow him. Could I do in sleep what I would not do when awake? I thought of Fout. The murders. Maybe Fout had a sleep disorder. Maybe he killed in a trance. He killed while he slept in his lower self. It wasn't himself that killed. He seemed awake, but it was a primitive self.

I prayed for Fout's wounds. His murders were his wounds. Christ died for his wounds, his murders. For once, I could stand in awe and wonder instead of horror at the unspeakable acts of Thomas Fout.

But the comfort soon left. I felt the turmoil again. The unruliness. My inability to take effective action.

Sometimes in church, I picked up on it when a man was addicted to pornography. I could feel that hot desire in the air, filling the room. The impression was pervasive. I knew when he had been on the Internet before he came to church. He was thinking of returning once he got home from church. He only wanted to be turned on again. But I didn't know what to do.

I thought I had been sensitive, and had been, to everything but murder. Fout had avoided my detection.

Mark Cabot: There Were Other Murders in Kansas

    I thought of the deprivation of some of my congregation. I thought of the abundance of the Saiths. I questioned God about the inequities. Had it affected Thomas Fout? Had he felt the poverty or plainness or the ineffectuality of his life and invented significance—a warped significance—power over the lives of others?

76

Grace Cabot
A Visit with Ruth Fout

The wife of Thomas Fout. The innocent sharer of his evil. The two were one. But she was different from him. *We are not one!* How she must have beat against that thought. The marriage was over. Ruth Fout was now Ruth Turner. But she could not return to who she was. She would be marked by Fout forever. What would be the name on her grave? Would her son keep his last name? Would Tom's brothers? His mother?

She came to the women's group occasionally for prayer, but she said little. Once she broke down, "I failed as a wife. I wasn't enough for him."

"Don't say that," I told her. "You couldn't keep him from that kind of evil."

How long would the news reporters follow her? Where could she go that they wouldn't follow? Had she accompanied her husband on his mission? How long would she be under suspicion? How long would she be the unwanted one people had to take into their houses to hide because they were Christian? How long could she live with others? Did they have a sign-up sheet? How could she live on her own without running to others?

Should she take some of the savings and rent a larger apartment? Would a landlord rent to her? Should she buy another house? She had money from the auction of their infamous house for much more than it was worth.

"They'll probably make a freak museum of it."

Ruth worried that she would be fired from her job after this interim. Why would they want her there again? Wouldn't her presence hurt business? Or maybe it would bring in gawkers. She had seen plenty of them.

"If you'd like, Mark will call your employer and assure him you knew nothing of the murders."

She nodded.

Zelda reached out her hand to comfort Ruth. I saw Zelda's fingers smudged with something. Dirt? No, it looked more like charcoal.

How frail their marriage had been. Ruth had lived it, experienced it as real, but Tom made it a mockery.

"The Lord is my shepherd I do not want," I heard Zelda say.

This earth, this ball where moments of eternal significance were decided by the most common and ordinary people.

77

Mark Cabot
The Saiths' Cabin by Themselves

Grace and I came to Orbson Lake during the week. Clare stayed in Buckholt with a school friend. We would leave before Roy and his family came for the weekend.

The evening sun shone on the metal roof of the boat dock as though it were a stone tablet. I sat on the porch by the bug light and wrote a letter to Thomas that I would never mail. I felt myself crossing into someplace I hadn't yet been in my depression.

"You shall not," the clay tablets from the mountain told you—but you did it anyway. I lost count of the times I wrote, "You shall not." I didn't stop writing until Grace came up behind me. There were times I went too far. There were times my thoughts felt unmanaged. Grace pulled me away from the table. I followed her to the dock. We got into the Saiths' boat. I started the motor and backed into the water. The evening sky above the water was huge with clouds.

"They're the souls of those Thomas Fout murdered," Grace said, making the same observation. "They're telling us they climbed to God. They're circling around his throne. Even the dogs and other animals he hurt are there. Maybe this earth is something easy to give up once you've seen God."

"I want to say that in heaven, those he murdered will let him run around them like a dog—I want to say that the animals he tortured will nip his feet for eternity."

Grace smiled but didn't say anything.

Mark Cabot: The Saiths' Cabin by Themselves

On the return to the cabin, the wind came up. The sky darkened. The water was choppy, then turbulent on the small lake. The waves were slate gray. They were like the veins of coal that the mining companies had strip mined in eastern Kansas along the Missouri border. The wind blew across them. The boat jumped the waves. I slowed the motor and yelled to Grace, asking if she were all right. She nodded her head.

"It's exhilarating."

In the past, she would have been leery of this adventure, too careful. She would not have allowed it at all if Clare had been with us. For a moment, something less apprehensive, more trusting opened in her. For a moment, I felt something that was intended for us. The day had been hot. Now it was cool. I nodded to her. After what we had been through, this was nothing.

Again, we drove the Saiths' boat onto the lake at night. This time it was dark. We let the motor idle. We let the boat drift. We would hear if another boat approached. We lay back in the dark and looked at the moon and the stars. I felt lifted from the boat into the dark and awful mystery of God.

Afterwards, I sat on the dock until nearly dark. I felt the instability of the lake. Yet it was held in its edges. A foot could step into it. But belly flop from the dock, and it was like landing on rock.

The lake was still as glass. I felt like I was sitting on the water. I heard the call of geese. I watched the way ducks moved in a steady line on the still water. The bugs flew in swarms above me. The absolute stillness. The clouds passing over. I was under the Almighty's hand.

The next day we walked on the road to get away from the noise. Builders were clearing trees for more houses and cabins. The smell of smoke from burning tree stumps was in the air. I could hear pounding, the distant sound of bulldozers and cement trucks. Orbson Lake would soon be overbuilt. Roy had bought some land near his lake house to keep others from clearing it.

Roy planned an addition on his lake house and his builders were there. Were the Saiths like the couple in 2 Kgs 4:9–10, who built a room for the prophet Elisha when he passed by their house? The only problem was that I was not Elisha. I felt that Roy was actually adding several rooms so that he could go to his lake house even when I was there. He seemed to know how necessary it was to me. I apologized to Roy for having to build another chamber, but he refused to accept my apology. He was building the addition because his children were getting older and wanted their friends to come. He even added a garage with a room above it.

On the road, Grace and I were surrounded by the autumn leaves. The trees pelted down acorns on us.

"We're under attack," I joked.

Grace didn't laugh.

78

Zelda Gheary
What a Little Box

What a skewed little world we lived in. What a little box Christianity was. Full of black swirls and continual paradoxes and misfits.

79

Mark Cabot
Fout

"Can you let go of the hate? Can you see Fout as a human being?" I asked Ralph Gheary when he came into the office on Tuesday. "Fout will be in prison until he dies."

"Would you have a service for him in the church when he dies in prison?"

"Yes," I said before I had time to think. "Fout lost everything. Family. Work. I think all he has left is God's forgiveness."

"I doubt if he is forgiven by everyone," Ralph said. "Ask the Oteros: Joseph, Julie, Josephine, Joseph II. Ask Kathryn Bright, Shirley Vian, Nancy Fox, Marine Hedge, Vicki Wegerle, Delores Davis . . . Were there others yet to be named?"

"You know the names—"

"I've prayed for their families. They are his victims too—the ones left behind. I stand for those who believe in Fout's sin."

Fout was afraid in prison.

"They would kill me if they could," he said when I visited.

"You're kept apart."

"They intimidate me with their looks," Thomas said. "I want out."

"I can't help you. I can pray for you, for your protection, for your remorse."

"Ruth never comes to see me."

"You feel abandoned by Ruth? Have you ever thought of what you've done to her?"

Sometimes in counseling when I saw someone doing something wrong, I let them go because I knew they wouldn't listen. They had to find out for themselves.

Is that why God had not intervened? Fout was going to murder anyway? That didn't make sense. Why did God let this happen? But the question still remained: Would God resurrect Thomas Fout? Would God accept Thomas Fout into his heaven?

"You've been to see him again," Grace said that evening.

We ate dinner, trying to make conversation. Clare saved the evening by talking about school. Her project. Her music lesson. Her homework.

Later that evening, I taped a message to Grace on our bathroom mirror. "I was in prison and you came to me."[1]

Maybe the Lord would open a prison ministry for me. But I didn't want that kind of ministry. I only wanted my own flock at Christ Church. It was all I could do to take care of them—their normal problems and dilemmas.

I thought of Thomas entering a house. I thought of his tactics—his maneuvers, tying up his victims, terrorizing them. Something got into my head he didn't like. I felt a smear of evil. I couldn't come away clean. The knowledge of evil. Was it what Adam experienced in the garden? The knowledge of *other*? Of something that didn't belong? An addition on a house that didn't work. That sucked heat into it and left the house cold. Something that could not be cleaned off. The daylight smeared with shadows.

The phone calls did not cease. Everyone was interested in the murderer. What did I know that others didn't or wouldn't say? I had been advised not to speak about it. Dr. Cole, the previous minister of Christ Church, called several times to see how I was doing.

"Why weren't the callers interested in normal Christianity?" I asked. "Was there a normal Christianity? God killed his Son and smeared his blood upon believers so he could see the blood and not them? What was normal about that?"

1. Matt 25:34–36.

God could forgive murder, but he could not forgive someone who did not believe in him? Could a murderer end up in heaven because he professed faith in Jesus Christ, while a good person who did not profess faith went to hell?

I was implicated by the fact that Thomas Fout was in my congregation—had been in my congregation. He was a sheep I was responsible for. But was he a sheep? What if the boundaries were not clear? It was not a question. It was a fact. I did not have the answers. I had semi-answers. Quasi-answers. Answers that I could come up with on my own. Common sense answers. Answers that seemed to be answers. I didn't like the quandary. I didn't like the place Thomas Fout had brought me to. I was to visit him in jail with mercy when I was not feeling merciful. When I was angry that Thomas had implicated me. When other ministers were asking me how I handled that one.

Jesus was found walking in the garden after the resurrection. Maybe there was a point to that. He reclaimed a place that had been created for us. We could re-enter in his name. I held on to that thought.

"The thought had been with me for years. It was my companion. I was duplicitous from the beginning," Thomas said on our next visit. "As a child, I found pleasure in hurting animals. Who could I tell? How could I tell you I wanted to murder? What would I say? How would I say it? What could you have done to prevent any of it? I would bring authorities down upon me."

"It would have been better than the murders you committed," I said. "Ten people would be alive, two of them children. Families would not be damaged, the children left without mothers. You would not be in prison."

"Well, all of that has happened. I can tell you now."

"Now that it's too late," I said. "But sometimes when I pray for you, it seems that you can be forgiven by God. He's been waiting to restore you to him."

"It's as easy as that?"

"I think that's what the Bible says," I answered. "I've been shaken by you until I'm not sure of anything."

"Do you forgive me yet?"

"Sometimes," I said. "Other times, the anger comes back."

"I'm sorry."

"It's a little late for that," I said. "Why did you find a fascination with murder?"

"It was an urge that just kept hitting me."

"You didn't find an abhorrence? It's what I find in you. It's hard for me to come here."

"I thought about murder. Over and over. I planned it. I carried out the plans. There was a precision I liked. It upset me when the murders got messy, as they occasionally did. Because I had not planned. Because something unexpected happened to the plans I had made. It became a trough I made. I walked in it. I couldn't get out."

"Did you want to?"

"Yes, there were times when I knew it was wrong."

"You are saying that like you knew it was wrong to get mad at a driver in front of you who wasn't going as fast as you wanted to go."

"There was a shift in my thinking. It suddenly felt all right to murder. It was something that had been given to me to do. It was my mission. I understood it once I was inside it."

I pulled away from Fout. I made an excuse and hurriedly left the prison.

Oh God, I prayed as I returned to Buckholt. I come to you in horror. I have said Fout's words about Christianity, "I understood it once I was inside it." I have said Fout's words about my own ministry, "There was a shift in my thinking. It suddenly felt right to minister." Was this world a trick? If the colored pieces of glass fell one way and then the other, it was still colored glass, no matter what pattern it made. I pulled off the road momentarily, overcome with the erasure of all I was. Were good and evil different sides of the same coin? Was everything relative, and we fell into whatever universe we spilled into?

I sobbed as I sat at the wheel. Maybe cars passed so quickly on the interstate that they wouldn't notice a man crying at the side of the road. Maybe the highway patrol would stop and drive me home. Maybe God would come and rebuild my faith.

The murders returned to my dreams. They came as constant replay. The authorities came to see me. Investigators. A lawyer. "You will be bombarded by calls," they said. I already had, I assured them. I was not to say anything.

"What do I know?" I said before the reporters. "Thomas Fout was a member of my congregation. He acted like anyone else. In fact, I wish others were as faithful in attendance and in taking up the duties of running the church as Thomas was."

What did I have to say? Nothing that anyone would be interested in.

The authorities helped me with a taped response on the answering machine: "The pastor is not available for interviews. He knows nothing about the murders and is not able to speak about Thomas Fout."

I sat by myself in my office. I listened to calls continue to come in. When the tape was full, it would reject further calls.

I had a cell phone to talk to my wife. The calls continued to come to the parsonage too. Sometimes a van stopped, and I knew the camera was on the church. I kept the doors locked. I didn't answer any knock on the door.

I read Scriptures. I prayed. I reminded myself of God's word.

I took notes as I read the book of Daniel one morning. Nebuchadnezzar was a murderer. He burned anyone who didn't worship him. He set up a large statue of himself and had people worship it. What a dictator he was. Yet God spoke to his heart, and he repented—once he had grown claws and eaten grass like an ox:

> At the end of the days, I, Nebuchadnezzar, lifted up my eyes unto heaven, and my understanding returned to me, and I blessed the Most High, and I praised and honored him who lives forever, whose dominion is an everlasting dominion, and his kingdom is from generation to generation.[2]

Maybe the dictator was given reprieve and was sitting in heaven singing with the angels. How unlikely was that? But the possibilities were there. Then why did I feel murky? A murderer could be restored.

But if the murderer murdered again . . . That was the problem in the question of Thomas Fout. Christian faith was often against human reason. It didn't always make sense. It didn't ever make sense, I wanted to think.

"Consider yourself in the oxen category at the present, eating grass in the field, humiliated, so to speak," I said to Thomas on another trip to Wyatt.

"Prison certainly is that."

"Your humiliation counts more to you than the suffering of your victims and their families? You may be eating more grass."

---

2. Dan 4:34.

Mark Cabot: Fout

"I will never get out of prison. Sometimes I think of the possibility of parole."

"I wouldn't hope too much for it."

"Maybe when I'm an old man. Maybe a judge would take pity."

"I doubt the public wants you with them."

80

Zelda Gheary
The Lock

I went to the hardware store and asked about a handyman. I called one of the names they gave me. He came to the house while Ralph was at the church. Ralph wouldn't notice. The lock was just a small opening in the knob where I would insert my key. Ralph seemed to stay clear of the room anyway. I mean, what did he want with the drawings I kept there?

One morning I nailed my *subworld* drawings to the walls. I stood back, nearly overcome with the landscape of hell and those in it trying to get out. I mean—all the morose desolation of the human race lined up in a mural.

What if my parents came for a visit? Or Ralph's family. No, I wouldn't let them. Ralph and I would go to Elwood. We would visit them.

What if one of Ralph's friends from the seminary stopped to see him and wanted to spend the night? But wasn't hell something that concerned them? I mean, wasn't it right up their alley?

81

Mark Cabot
The Bookshelf

For some reason, the book always caught my eye. Maybe because the D's on the spines of my Dostoyevsky were eye-level when I turned in my chair. I should be reading the Bible or Martin Luther or Saint Augustine. I took *The Brothers Karamazov* from the shelf. I reread some of my notes and underlining: "If anything . . . does regenerate and transform the criminal, it is only the law of Christ speaking in the conscience." Maybe that's why Thomas made himself visible, sending a disk to the newspaper that he knew could be traced. Even when he asked if it could and they said it couldn't, he must have known the authorities could retrieve the deleted information that listed his church duties. Maybe it was Christ speaking in his conscience. I returned to this because I needed to. I needed to get it clear in my mind—going over it and over it to hold it there. Christ did have his hand on Thomas Fout. He brought him to justice. But I returned to the problem. If Thomas Fout had Christ speaking in his conscience, how could he have murdered?

I read Dostoyevsky's whole chapter on church and state. How could Russia let that slip away? No, they extinguished it.

Had I foreseen somehow within myself what I would go through? Had I known I would deal with this problem in public, openly, before the whole nation? In time, people would forget. I didn't need to worry about my inflated importance. It was temporary. Someday, people would look, and they would know there was something familiar about me, but it would take a while before that look of recognition would come across their faces and they would peg me as the minister with the criminal in his congregation.

Dostoyevsky believed that a state punished, and a church forgave. Yes, a criminal could have faith. But did the crime negate faith? No, but did the crime negate the criminal's standing before God? The Scriptures were clear about God's justice. They were clear about his forgiveness. But how could I reconcile those two oppositions?

I was angry that Thomas Fout made me confront thoughts and questions I didn't want to confront.

A Christian could commit a crime. A Christian could commit multiple crimes. Salvation was not a stop-gate from wrongdoing. All things were possible. Even murder. What God was this that permitted such freedom of will? Why did he permit Thomas Fout to live and allow Tessa to die?

"Are you there, God?" I wanted to yell, but I kept quiet. I didn't want to startle my secretary. I didn't want her or Ralph to know I faced doubt laced with such deep anger that I closed the book and wept in the closet in my office, stifling my sobs in one of my minister's robes.

Should I stop visiting Thomas Fout in prison? Wasn't I his prisoner? Didn't he have me on a short leash, pulling me to prison to visit him—to give him the outlet and solace that I was denied? I would make Grace happier if I didn't go. But according to my ministry, I had to.

I looked through Dostoyevsky again. I reread the chapter "Peasant Women Who Have Faith." They were the women Father Zossima came to bless. They wailed hopelessly before him because of the endless hardship of their lives. There was one particular woman who lost a child: "Rejoice, for your little one is with the Lord." Or was it, "She is with the angels singing before God"? I had wanted one of them on Tessa's grave, but Grace wouldn't hear of it. What had upset her about those passages?

I read another chapter because I felt there were the instructions for me. I was to see Thomas as a precious son. I felt reviled as I thought of Fout as precious. *The Brothers Karamazov* wasn't Scripture. But the truth within that book spoke to me. I continued to read and to underline passages.

What waited in the afterlife for Thomas Fout? That was up to God.

In the book of Revelation, the different churches received different rewards. If a murderer could go to heaven, wouldn't that be the reward? That they weren't in hell where they belonged? How could Thomas Fout be in heaven with others who had not acted upon their impulses—who had felt murder or adultery, but had never acted on it? Who prayed to God, and through the Holy Spirit, received strength to forego their desires? Was it possible? Maybe Fout would be just inside the door, so barely in that his robe caught in the door each time it opened.

It was a fearful world where Thomas Fout had stepped. The world of demons and evil. Maybe Christ would keep him from being swallowed. Fout sat in the state prison at Wyatt in the fear and discomfort of his incarceration. He had his murders to think about. Maybe now he knew how his victims felt. But what did he think? Did he review his *accomplishments*? Is that how he saw them, getting away with murder for years? The authorities would not have caught him, if he had kept quiet. But the murders he committed cried out for revenge. He gave himself up by a stupid act, erasing files and sending the disk to the newspaper office that had turned it over to the police. He had to see how far he could go. He believed the police liked his game, but they did not. They were repulsed by Thomas Fout. They wanted him caught and convicted. They wanted justice. They wanted it over.

I read *The Grand Inquisitor* again. The problem with freedom was that it came with free will. There it was again—the free will that caused the trouble. Freedom came with the ability to act, to make choices, to plot. If I preached the best sermons and served the best potluck at church suppers, I would have the most people in my church. That was the thinking of my free will. But was it the way God intended me to use my freedom? What did he want me to do in the face of Thomas Fout? Use my freedom to think of ways to redeem the church? To defend it?

"I think you're mixing free will with instinct for survival," Ralph said when I recommended the book to him.

"Don't we have the same instinct? Those of us raised in church are held in place by belief in God's rules and in the reward for following those rules. We are free to do otherwise if we want to risk what we believe. We are free to acknowledge that we are free men in an absurd world."

"But are we free?" Ralph asked. "I have been enlightened by God. I cannot act on my own. I know better not to. I trust God to lead me. Otherwise I make mistakes. And is this world absurd?" Ralph asked, "If it is the world God created, and not our own actions?"

"Wait until you have lost a child—after all the prayer you are capable of. After your congregations and other congregations of the clergy you know are praying. Yet God turns his back and removes your child from your house. Wait until you are torn apart."

"Just as we have freedom, God has freedom to do what he wants," Ralph said. "He is wrapped in mystery. How unforgivable to lose a child."

"It's the first question I'll ask when I stand before him," I said. "Why she was taken."

"Yes, you're full of righteous indignation," Ralph said. "You've suffered an injustice. I agree. But you're before one who doesn't have to answer to you. I would be careful. I think our first job will be to fall down before God in awe and praise."

Ralph looked weary as he stood before me in my office. I was sorry I argued with him.

"Of course," I agreed, subdued for a moment, "but you have freedom. When you want to kill Thomas Fout, you have freedom not to do it. They may do it in prison. Who knows what is ahead for Thomas Fout? Who knows the terror he faces in prison?"

What words Dostoyevsky wrote. I looked at the passages I had marked. Father Superior with devils under his cossack, in his pockets, hanging from his neck. There was even a devil hiding behind the door with a long tail: "[I] slammed the door, pinching his tail in it."

Where would the bad spirits be hiding in Fout, I wondered. In his heart? They were all over the prison. I was sure. I left Dostoyevsky on my desk to open another day. It was my own shirt pocket from which I felt the horns poking. Could we have been left in greater confusion and suffering than you caused, O Fout, laying on us so many cares and unanswerable problems?

82

Ralph Gheary
Bicycle

I watched Zelda become more concerned with her art. I wanted her to let it go. I wanted to tell her it was not appropriate. But I had to stand back. I saw that she needed to draw. What were those dark, swirling marks she made? What purpose did they serve? I had to let her go. I wasn't used to tolerating what I couldn't handle, but Buckholt had changed all that. Sometimes I saw the women look at Zelda from their distance in church. I had married my wife to help her be her own person. She would return to herself. When this crisis passed.

The visits to the prison at Wyatt were a testimony to other prisoners. The church did not abandon its own. We were sticklers. We had murderers among us. Christ died for the ungodly. To enter Christianity was to abandon all hope of reason and propriety. We were fools for Christ. I was in a place I least wanted to go to. Outside my understanding. Off-balance. I wanted decorum. I wanted predictability. A secure place in the hope of Christ. That's what I wanted. Not to be ripped apart by the consequences of murder.

Sometimes at night, I was aware of an old ache in my leg. I had broken it in grade school when I fell from a bicycle. I was racing with a friend, looked away for a moment, and the wheel ran against the curb. When I tried to straighten the bike, it slammed to the ground. I tried to brace the fall with my left leg, but my foot twisted. I heard the snap of bone before I felt it. I remembered the sun in my eyes. I remembered light. I remembered holding my leg, my friend laughing that I fell until he realized I was hurt. A woman came from her house. She had called the ambulance. A small crowd gathered. I remembered the pain then as they lifted me from the ground onto the stretcher. My mother was at the hospital. Then my father. The anesthesia made me sleep. Afterwards, I remembered the throbbing of my leg. Friends drew on my cast. Some just signed their name, but one friend drew a bicycle with his ballpoint pen. Above the bike, someone else had signed their name, and the ink blurred so it looked like a large ball was riding the handlebar. I remembered looking at the drawing of the bike when my foot was raised. It was somehow meaningful. As if there was a sun above the darkness of the accident. No, it didn't make sense, but it connected me to something I needed. There it was: art. I could say it was art that got me through.

83

Mark Cabot
The Struggle with Sin

From time to time, it caught up with me all over again. How could I face the people's stares? How could I have not known that I harbored a murderer?

Grace and I prayed, and I felt stronger. How many of my congregation were left? How did they wake in the morning with the thought of Fout between them?

I went into my study and opened the Bible. "Whoever is born of God does not sin."[1] How I hated that verse. I felt born of God, yet I sinned. Therefore, was I not born of God? No, I was made of flesh. I would sin all my life. What was my sin? I was not trusting. I was fearing. I was letting Fout get to me. I was reliving the shame. I was angry with God that this was the valley he led me through. I did not want it.

I named my sin: mistrust of God.

Sin was there like the moon. It was a lesser light to follow. It was there, varying in its light. Sometimes dull in the sky. Sometimes behind the clouds. Sometimes bright. No, that analogy didn't work. The moon caught light reflected from the sun. Sin was not of God. But God had created Satan. Satan had fallen from the light. The moon left the sun, fell away from it, to be its own light, but couldn't—

---

1. 1 John 3:9.

My thinking was flawed. There were subtle ways that dealing with Fout's murders had taken a toll. Would I be able to reason again? Had I ever been a scholar? Hadn't I tried several things before the ministry? Hadn't I scavenged? No, I had been chosen to be a pastor. I had to believe God. Maybe I could leave the silliness of my reasoning behind. No, I was given free will. I was given thought. But I could not think my way through this. I could not think my way to God. He was beyond my thoughts. I could not reach God with my understanding.

Grace was too thin. She had the look of someone trying to hold their appetite so no one would know how large it would be if it were let loose. There was a self-consciousness to it. She had a steady control over herself. She did not like change. See what change had brought to us all. She was the pastor's wife. A difficult job in a difficult situation.

The struggle with sin was like mowing the lawn again and again. Every time I looked, the grass had grown taller. I worked during the year, trimming bushes, spraying for weeds. People staring as they drove by.

84

Grace Cabot
A Reminder

My husband reminded me I was a rational woman. When the wilderness came, I read Scripture again: the words of a treacherous God who took daughters by illness and families by murder. Who turned his back on his own Son on the cross. Who made good of it by bringing him back to life. God could do that. Yes, he could. But he didn't do it often. There was a sick girl in the Bible, the daughter of Jairus in Matt 9:18. Jesus called her back to life. But not Tessa Margaret Cabot. No, she rose to heaven. Even I could not call her back. But even I could carry grudges. No, I had to let them go. I didn't have room.

Maybe I would have lunch with Ruth Fout. We were both betrayed by men, if God could be considered a man. I was surprised Mark hadn't asked me if I had lunch with Ruth. It was part of my Christian duty—to remind Ruth of her place of security in God. But Ruth had a job. She had money from the auction of their house. She lived in an apartment. Her children were grown and lived other places, but they were both alive. She continued at the job she had held while Tom was murdering. No, he wasn't murdering for many years. I had to be fair.

85

Mark Cabot
A Little Wind Blows in Kansas

Once it had been something different—before I knew Thomas Fout murdered. I was as yet spared the horror. I wanted that time back. I knew it would never return. Time had changed into Before Thomas Fout and After Thomas Fout. There were questions asked that I couldn't answer. There were embarrassments. Rages. I was impatient. Short-tempered. I couldn't face my situation, but I had to. As a minister, I knew that in Christ there was strength for me in all things. I was the pastor of a murderer. It hurt to the bottom of my being. I was marked. I was set apart. In meetings, I could feel them looking at the back of my head. I could feel the sting of their stare. I cowered before it. When I woke in the morning, the dread of the day was upon me. I got up. Showered. Grace fixed toast and an egg for me. I got in my car. Neighbors saw me back from my drive. "Poor man," they were saying. Poor minister who had his church smeared with murder. How could he face the public? How could I face the public? Christ was my strength, as I said. It made me self-conscious. I was aware of every step, every word, every action. I could not move unconsciously among people. I was on the spot, and the spot kept growing. How could I stop it? Diminish it? Sometimes I felt my hands shake. Sometimes I was so tired I went to bed as soon as it grew dark. Sometimes Clare was still finishing homework, or Grace was still in the kitchen when I felt the unbearable exhaustion. Grace was brittle. Was I any less so? I couldn't share the weight with her. She could hardly bear her own weight. She buried herself in housework and grocery lists. She was holding on any way she could. Fout had separated us also. He murdered us also, or had murdered the lives we once had.

I used to worry about my stand on abortion, on stem cell research, on evolution, on our military invasion of another country. What would I say when asked? What did I think when no one was asking? Had I thought through these things? Or had I tried to walk the thin line around them? There was no walking around this one. Now I wondered about God's mercy on the sinner from my congregation. Fout had diminished the horrors going on in other parts of the world, even the suffering people in Iraq and Pakistan. I felt that sometimes when I prayed, I picked up distant cries.

Then Ralph was in my office saying something about God not mixing with evil, "He kills all that is not his," referring to God's command to Israel to kill all the tribes in their way when they claimed the promised land.

"It could mean something else—" I said.

"Anything you don't want to believe, you say is symbolic," Ralph told me.

"Yet I believe Fout is redeemed," I said.

"I do not," Ralph said.

"Maybe he will be inside heaven without reward."

"Surely not with reward. But I doubt he is there," Ralph said.

"What if, when the victims died, they saw a vision beyond anything that could be imagined? Would it be all right then?" I asked.

"No, because of those left behind, stunned, confused, angry."

When Ralph left my office, I picked out the opening hymn, *To God Be the Glory* by Fanny Crosby, 1875, "the vilest offender who truly believes that moment from Jesus a pardon receives."

I decided on the Scripture for the bulletin: "Faith comes by hearing and hearing by the word of God."[1] But Fout remained vile after he believed, if he believed. He believed he believed. And I believed he did.

I was suspicious of everyone. What were they doing behind my back?

Were they considering my removal like Pluto had been removed from the list of planets?

I went with a group of men to the prison to visit Thomas: Roy Saith, Ralph, Jack Kester, Ben Ramos, and Albert Furnish.

---

1. Heb 10:17.

"For the word of God is living, and powerful, and sharper than any two-edged sword, piercing even to the dividing asunder of soul and spirit, and of the joints and marrow, and is a discerner of the thoughts and intents of the heart. Neither is there any creature not manifest in his sight, but all things are naked and opened unto the eyes of him with whom we have to do."[2]

"If you want to be terrorized, just think about that."

I looked at Fout, thinking of this grave he put me in, this cement block I was buried under. But God promised that everything that could be shaken would be shaken.[3]

What positive would come from it? It pushed Scripture into my life. For every wedge Fout drove into my faith, I searched for Scripture to fill it.

---

2. Heb 4:12–13.
3. Heb 12:26.

86

Ralph Gheary
What's in the Locked Room?

"What's in the locked room?"

Zelda didn't answer.

"I didn't know there was lock on that door."

"What's in there you need?"

"I want to see what's in the room."

"It's my workroom. My own place. You have your office at the church. I don't go through your papers."

"I don't have any papers you can't see."

"I respect your privacy," Zelda said.

"What does that have to do with it?" I asked. "When did we start having locks on doors?"

"I have drawings that would upset you. They're my *subworld* drawings. You've seen enough of them. I know you don't like them. You're always telling me to stop drawing. To get over it."

"I know you need to draw."

"If my drawings were flowers, or landscapes . . ." Zelda said. "But these are of the *subworld*."

"What *subworld*?"

"My *subworld* drawings. You've seen them—the place Thomas Fout brought us to. I had to work through the darkness. I had to draw the possibilities of hell when I thought of the *horror* of it all. He instilled something in me I had to draw. It was horrific. It was unworldly. Yet it was exactly the world when I thought of history."

"Let me see this *horror*."

"I have them on the wall. I don't want you to see what I've done."

"Zelda, you act as if there's a monster in there."

"There is."

"I want the key."

"I don't want to give it to you."

"Where is it?"

Her shoulder bag was on the table—the metal typewriting table she took from her grandmother's house. She kept it by the door. I went through the bag and found her key ring. On it was one small key I didn't recognize. I opened the door. I stood in the doorway, stunned. I was horrified. I saw the drawings started across the ceiling. I felt her behind me.

"Zelda, you need help . . . Are you ill? They're awful. They're frightening. You couldn't have done them. What if someone saw them? They have to be covered. I'll buy paint tomorrow. How can I sleep in the next room with this hell in here? This pit?"

Zelda came at me with the anger I saw at her grandmother's funeral when I first received the call about Thomas Fout. "Leave them alone," she demanded. "They're my drawings. I want them on the wall—I want them across the ceiling. I'm not finished with them yet. I can track them with Scripture. Don't you know the Old Testament wrath?"

I listened to her pleas. I left the room. I closed the door. I locked it again. I put the keys back in her purse on the typing table. I went outside. I stood in the front yard and looked into the distance. For the first time, I wondered who I had married.

87

Zelda Gheary
Aftermath

I felt uncovered. Not from clothing, but my thoughts were showing as if I was without a skull. What had Jesus gone through on the cross as sin ate him—as the forces that struggled against God attacked him also? What did he go through as God turned his back on him, so the awful sin of humanity would cover him and he would suffer a suffering no one could imagine? He became a black hole sucking all the sin of humanity into him. And the blackness outside his Father. What was the world that could carry what I drew? The invisible world made visible.

Christ was marred beyond recognition on the cross, crosshatched with a drawing pencil that smeared the page. Jesus entered evil. Became it. Let it move over him. I don't want to be in a place where I would have to sit next to Thomas Fout. That can't be. I was stabbing my *subworld* drawing, leaving the heavy construction paper pocked with holes, broken into, warped beyond recognition. The wounds of thorns—the sword that cut into the side of Christ as his holy being took on sin and opened all its horrendous chambers, from which no one could escape because it was the world that sin had made and there was nothing else. It chose to live away from God. I worshipped Christ, who was slashed on the cross for my sin.

88

Mark Cabot
The Core of Evil

Here I am with a rope around my wrists. Here I am, pulled by an event. The murders committed by Thomas Fout. It was he who was leading me. A minister who was also a friend suggested that I fast when I was depressed. I knew the Scriptures about fasting and prayer. I know the Lord fasted. I made it through the first day without eating, then ate the next morning. Grace said she didn't like to hear my stomach growl. She felt like she wasn't doing her job of feeding me.

I could not tolerate more deprivation. I had to have my routine. "I am weak. I am weak," I prayed in my office.

I learned there were questions I would not ask.
"Grace, do you believe in God?"
"I believe in a God I cannot trust."
What darkness we felt in those days. We were shut in a box. Would it ever be opened? I had to remain functioning. Nothing was safe. But I could know that Thomas Fout had the judgment ahead, as did I—as did I.

When Martin Luther entered the monastery, he said, "You see me now, but not ever again." The man he was at the time would change.

Mark Cabot: The Core of Evil

Each morning, I read a different section of Luther, hoping to get through the day on his words. Martin Luther offered Christians assurance. He was concerned with the Turks, the plague, the purging of transgressions. When I first read Luther, he was not what I expected. He was too flawed, too fleshy. For some reason, Zelda Gheary came to mind as I read.

Luther continually worried about how he could please God. How he could know anything, stumbling blindly along. That's how God left us on earth.

I read that Luther had also lost a daughter.

Was I spending too much time in my office reading? What was Grace doing with her time? Why didn't I ask her?

How could anyone be free of sin and the fear of death? That was Luther's concern. How could anyone function?

Despair was a benefit. That was my conclusion after reading Luther. Since I knew despair, I needed that thought. I was not alone in my faith. The Christian was a servant. The Christian was free. These oppositions were ever before me. Was it the thesis I would nail to the door?

Night was the worst. My dreams steamed with fear. It loosened any adhesive with which I held myself together. If Thomas Fout was capable of murder, then I was. That thought was terrifying. I could not trust myself to behave as a Christian. If the right circumstances came about, I could murder also. That's what it meant. Was Grace safe beside me? Was Clare safe in her bed in the next room? Was Tessa's death my fault?

Once I woke, heart pounding, afraid someone was in my house. I sat up in bed, listening for a while. I heard nothing. I got up slowly. I didn't want to wake Grace. I went downstairs, but no one was there. I sat for a while in the green chair in my in the dark.

I wrestled with God and got my faith out of joint. Why were things the way they were? Surely a loving God would make a safer world. He would not let the brutalities happen, but he sent his Son to the cross. He let people go to hell. He told Israel to go into Canaan and kill the enemy tribes. Maybe Fout thought he was carrying out God's command.

"I've been reading Martin Luther again," I told Tom when I saw him at Wyatt. "He says that penance is an inward turning. I don't see that in you."

"I'm sorry I murdered. I'm sorry for the families that have suffered. But there's nothing I can do about it now."

"You'd still be out there with your 'projects,' as you call them, if you weren't in prison."

"I might have decided to abandon them."

"No, Tom, you wouldn't," I insisted.

"I didn't for all those years—"

"I've heard you say more than once you had your next victim in sight," I reminded him.

What did I do to deserve this? I came to a church with murder in its history. It was up to me to deal with it. The former pastor went into hiding. I felt it was unfair. But then I thought about the unfairness of the cross: a righteous man, Jesus, suffered more than I could ever know.

"I don't understand how you could sit in church after you had murdered," I said.

"Have you murdered?" Fout asked.

"No."

"You don't know what it's like. It is absorbing. Once I picked it up, I couldn't put it down. I wanted to do it again. It stayed with me. It was a partner. It became a desire that was stronger than I could defeat. It was with me. It *was* me. I was in it night and day. I dreamed of murder. I would wake in the morning. I had been with my lover, murder. I had to have it. It was glorious."

Thomas' face became livelier the more he talked. He saw murder as a game. A task. A hunt. Look at him. He was alive with murder.

"I can't hear any more of this, Tom," I said. "I have to leave. I can't hear any more at the moment."

Mark Cabot: The Core of Evil

The possibility of depravity. That's what I picked up when I visited Thomas Fout: the terrifying bottom of the human mind. I couldn't share this with Grace. I didn't even want to sleep in the same bed. I was afraid I would infect her.

It was a windy day as I drove back to Buckholt. On an overpass, a fist of wind shoved my car. I thought for a moment I was going off the road on a bridge over a river. I thought of the car falling into the water and me unable to get out of the car. I thought of suffocating. Of not being able to breathe. I thought of drowning. I was caught under the oppressive weight of Fout. I could drive off the road and end it. Then he could not bother me anymore. I longed for it to be over. I longed to feel the car drift off the road. It would be easy. But something held me to the road. Something brought me back to my senses. I was under the oppressive weight of Christ. Even the crackling peace of his knowledge had sharp edges.

There were other times I felt someone was on the road behind me. I looked back several times, but no one was there. I didn't tell Grace what I was thinking.

At night I slept in a jungle. A street was nothing like a veldt. A street was nothing like a verdict. But there had not been a trial. Fout had been his own judge and jury. He had usurped a trial and national attention on his deeds. No, he would be in control. There was something self-centered in sin. Sin didn't care who it hurt. Sin was manipulative.

My will be done—not yours. Maybe that was the core of evil.

Where were my thoughts going? They jutted against one another—truncating one another—cutting the other off—amputating. I felt the terror of my thoughts. They were saw blades after one another. Maybe I was losing my mind. Maybe I had lost my mind and was only imagining Thomas Fout. How could I trust anything except the terror that stalked me?

I imagined a cartoon for the newspaper. Murder found in the pew. "Who is sitting beside you on Sunday morning?" written in a bubble coming from their mouths.

I could write the psalm of the defeated.

89

Zelda Gheary
Places We Should Not Go

> In searching for the bedrock.
> —Rosalind Krauss, *Under Blue Cup*

There were places we should not go. But Thomas Fout took us there. He sought out the places, entered them, and would not leave.

90

Ralph Gheary
Calculation

There are those in the congregation who asked how they could believe in a God who would send people to hell. They wanted to believe the cross was not really necessary. If the Jews had accepted Christ, he would not have had to go to the cross. The roots of hell were in trying to figure out a way around the cross.

91

Mark Cabot
Reconciliation

I picked up Saint Augustine and tried to read again—a little further along. Book 7, chapter 5, "God's Omnipotence and the Fact of Evil": "Where then is evil, and . . . by what means has it crept in here? What is its root, and what is its seed?" Augustine continues to question the source of evil. And the reason. God was not powerless. Yet evil remained.

As I read, I made my own questionings to God, but they were delivered in the form of statements: I am mad that I've been set up. You, O God, knew Thomas Fout was here when I consented to come to this church. You could have warned me in a dream, in some way—in any of the ways you have of letting us know. How often I have brought my depression before you, and often you have done nothing. Yet I'm sustained. When Tessa died, I was angry. You could have healed her and restored her to life. Why do children die? Innocent children with the full hope of life before them—with the promise of a godly life. She seemed willing to give up her life. She didn't rail against you, O God. After her death, I would return to the closet in my office and cry. Grace likewise had her place to go and grieve by herself. We helped Clare grieve. We all grieved together. We comforted ourselves with psalms. What could hurt after the death of a beloved child full of promise? Did you not see how she loved school? How she loved church? She would have been your servant all her life. Yet you took her and let Thomas Fout live. A murderer at Christ Church. Who would have believed this trick of God?

Mark Cabot: Reconciliation

In seminary I believed that you loved us. That you ordered our steps. That you were our Father and the giver of good gifts. What have I received from you? Am I allowed to question? It seems you are displeased with me. If I have a secret sin, if there is something I am not aware of, would you bring it to my attention rather than continue to punish? To torture me with the loss of another child? I ask that you leave me this one—Clare. I would ask why there were no more children, if you were going to take one of our two. I would ask, between Thomas Fout and the death of a child, doesn't the greater evil seem the loss of a child?

Am I without any will of my own? Don't you give us free will? If I had free will, I would have not lost a daughter. I would not have come to Christ Church. I would have let someone else take the rap. I would have let someone draw the losing ticket to this pastorate. I would have left it to someone else to explain why they had a murderer in their midst and never knew it. Why they never saw the slightest clue of what Fout had done. We were *friends*. If you asked me who was a faithful member of my congregation, I would have said Thomas Fout. We talked in my office. It wasn't a counseling session, though maybe it should have been, but I liked to visit with him. Our families did not get together. Maybe Tom was jealous of the time we spent with the Saiths, but our children were the same ages as the Saiths.' You would think I would have had some inkling, but there was nothing. *Nothing.* How could you have let me be so blind? How could you have led me on this path? I can grieve with the families of the victims because I have lost a beloved member of my family. I have seen the passing of my parents, but I have also *lost* my child. Fout killed two children. He tried to kill others.

I was prostrate on the floor, as I had been for my ordination—seeking God's will for my ministry. I was confessing my hatred of the bitter waters I had been given. I would rather have sat smugly with my congregation watching someone else handle this one. I would rather not be the one holding the bag. I looked for answers, and there were none there. You left stories of healing in the Bible to torture me. In Scripture you brought people back to life. Lazarus was an old man. You healed Jairus' daughter, yet you took Tessa away from me. Though I live, I have seen death. I have been unable to get up off the floor. I am grateful that this closet is in this office. I am grateful I can fit into this closet. I am grateful that I can lie facedown in this closet. Who had thought to make the pastor's closet the length of a man's body? The floor was more or less the size of a coffin. Just a little longer and wider. Maybe another minister gave the advice to the architect. Maybe there had not been a closet before, and a minister in the past had it built—I would ask Reverend Cole.

I was grateful that I was a minister with mud on my face. Ink on my hands. How many words does it take to unravel—to reveal the way I feel, Lord? You already know. But I want to tell you in case you have been busy elsewhere while all of this was going on. I know there are wars in other parts of the world. I know men are dying. I know there is terror and torture and all the evil humanity can do. I know others are ready to explode. I am grateful there is a light bulb at the end of the string so I can read in this closet. Have mercy upon me, O Lord, for I am weak. O Lord, heal me. I'm weary of my groaning; all the night I make my bed to swim. I continued to read Ps 6. Its verses floated on the floodwaters.

I am distraught, O Lord. I wish I could be like Job and trust you in the worst of this loss.

Were we growing a little dull and slow, Lord? You decided to pick up the pace?

Why do you stand far away, O Lord? Why do you hide yourself in times of trouble?[1]

I got the *Lives of Saints* from my bookshelf. I heard my secretary talking in the outer office. Who was the other voice? It was a man. I couldn't recognize his words. I heard my secretary laugh. They were visiting about something. It wasn't serious. I didn't know the man. But I had not recognized a murderer when he sat in my congregation. I had an "In Prayer" sign on my door I had placed there after the arrest of Thomas Fout. My secretary knew not to disturb me.

I returned to my closet, where I read, sitting with my back against the wall. I thought that next time I would bring a folding chair.

There he was, yes, it was him. Them, rather: Jonas and Barachisius, who were martyred in AD 326 and 327. Jonas was flogged. He was then bound and left in the winter night. Barachisius was told that Jonas had renounced his faith. When he didn't believe them, they poured hot pitch over his body and hung him by one foot in the cold night. Jonas likewise was told that Barachisius had renounced his faith. His fingers and toes were cut off. His bones broken. He was thrown into a vat of hot pitch. Barachisius was impaled, and hot pitch was poured down his throat. Who had done that? King Sapor II in Persia. I suppose now he was staked and roasting in

---

1. Ps 10:1.

hell. I suppose now he felt hot tar in his throat. I closed the book. I knelt in silence before the living God who impaled my heart upon him.

It was a matter of perspective. Thomas Fout was a novice in the light of this.

"Who was the man in the office?" I asked my secretary when I finished reading in the closet.

"The UPS man. He delivered a book you ordered."

What had I learned from my time in prayer? That my prostrate body would fit in the closet in my office. Evil was something I feared. The very thought of it made me tremble.

There were times when I knew Grace wanted to return to McPherson. Her family was a solace to her. I could feel her longing for escape. Sometimes I thought that she felt Tessa still needed her. Grace and I were polite to one another. Overly polite. Clare made up for it by making more noise than usual, turning up her music. She was hoping we would reprimand her, which we did. Maybe Grace was hoping to break the false cordiality that was suffocating us. I was afraid of her frailty. It was a presence between us. We had been together in a new intimacy, raw and startling. We had been so far into each other's privacy that we had to draw back. We had to return to normal. Return to a couple who had a murderer in their church. What was there about that to get upset? We had crossed a line of *ours*, back to hers and mine. We were afraid to look too clearly, afraid to touch, wanting intimacy but feeling it was wrong because we felt like strangers to this new knowledge. Not going forward, but retreating. I couldn't push it. At times, I saw a look in her eyes and knew she was close to tears. It was making her angry that I saw it. Sometimes her eyes were red, watery. She might have been crying out of sight, or so near crying that the tears gathered just before falling.

I think she wanted to sleep in another room, the empty bedroom, but that had been Tessa's. Grace seemed to stay on her side of the bed, disappearing into the covers. I couldn't let her disappear. I had to seek her out—finally have a confrontation. She was not going to disappear from me.

"Do you want to go to counseling?"

"Would that make Fout go away?" she asked.

"We have a cross to bear."

"We've had more than one of them."

"It will be easier if we both carry the weight together," I said.

"I've let you down."

"Don't be sure about that. I need you, Grace. Come back to me."

"I am back."

"No, you aren't. You're absent from me. Let me hold you."

I put my arms around her. She felt unyielding at first. She was on a far island. I was on mine. I would reach across and pull hers toward mine. We had knowledge of the intimacy of our marriage. I wanted us to reach it again.

92

Thomas Fout
Save Me, O God

Mark left a Bible with me at one of our first meetings. I sat in my cell and read. "Save me, O God, for the waters have come up to my neck."[1] I put my finger in the pages of Ps 69 and thought for a moment. I assured myself I could not be executed. The death laws were repealed during the years I murdered.

I continued to read—I sink in the mire. Once I got stuck on a muddy road. I remembered I had to get out of the car and walk through the mud to call a truck.

Don't let me sink. Don't let them get ahold of me. The fear of them is upon me. Don't let the floodwater overflow me, or let the deep swallow me up. Turn to me according to the multitude of your mercies. Do not hide your face from me. I am in trouble. You know my reproach. I am full of heaviness. I look for someone to take pity, and there is no one. "They gave me gall for my food, and for my thirst they gave me vinegar to drink."[2] That was the voice of Christ bound up in David's sufferings. "Let them be blotted out of the Book of the Living, and not be written with the righteous."[3] Do not blot me out of the Book of the Living, O God, do not blot. "Remove his name from the Book of Life"—that's what was written

---

1. Ps 69:1.
2. Ps 69:21.
3. Ps 69:28.

about Judas, who hanged himself after betraying Christ.[4] Forgiveness was there. I'm convinced of it. He didn't take what was offered, but I took the forgiveness God offered.

Those who hate me are more than the hairs of my head. They are mighty who would destroy me. My sins are not hidden from you. I have become a stranger to my brothers, an alien to my mother's children. My brother hardly writes from Iraq. Many of my family do not visit me. Those who sit in the gate speak against me. Deliver me out of the mire.

God, you know what I have done. I ask forgiveness. You know what I felt when I had their lives in my hands. You know what power is. I felt I have held your hand. I could create. I could extinguish. You as well as I.

I'm a murderer condemned to prison. I confessed to the murders. There was no trial. I handled that. What am I going to do? How do I face the terror at night when it comes? I know there is room for me in the border of Christianity. I would call it the confines of Christianity.

I felt the pulse in their necks with my fingers. I could slow it, or let it speed ahead. I remember the pulsing. I felt an awakening when I went into their bedrooms. I was giving them fire. I was a boy and someone was setting me on fire. They were showing me where it was. I didn't know how to turn it off. I didn't want to. I wanted to feel the swift, burning rise. There would be strict enforcement of the law. The pulsating. I look for someone to take pity. How that seemed like the voice of one of my victims.

There were times in dreams when I saw it again.

There were times when my selective readings of the Scriptures did not work.

I look for Ruth to visit. Or my children. Well, Mark Cabot comes. Sometimes, someone who wants to write a book. Or interview me. Or make a film. Someone who wants to know what is in my mind. Who wants to take my name and cover it with theirs. They have their own gain in mind. Often, I get letters, most of them unfavorable. Do they know what it is to defend myself? Now I go to court. The judge says I can't make money from any movie or book written about me. Maybe I can tell them what it is like. I can tell them my regrets. Do they know what it's like to know there are people who want me to go howling into the abyss? Do they know how it feels never to be able to drive through a neighborhood again?

4. Rev 3:5.

93

Mark Cabot
Tessa Again

When Martin Luther lost Magdalene, his daughter, he wrote, *Du Liebes Lenichen*, "You will rise and shine like the stars and sun." You are well while I am sorrowful. Luther also always seemed to be thinking of himself.

I got up from the chair at my desk in my office and went into what had become my chamber of prayer and anguish. In the blackness of my closet, I was back in Tessa's hospital room on the night of her death. How could God have invented something so despicable as life? I was the pastor, the father. I should have spoken words of assurance. Yet Tessa was the one ministering to me. When I sat with her, I felt I sat before God. I still carried the image of the white sheet and her white face against the white sheet. The darkness surrounded us, yet it was the light I remembered. I remember thinking the brightness of her hurt my eyes.

We had hoped she would live. We knew God heard our prayers. The whole church met for prayer. The whole district. The calls and messages and letters arrived daily. They were praying. In God there was hope. And for a moment, we saw hope. Until the afternoon the doctor called us aside, and hope passed. His words delivered to us the inevitable. God heard our prayers, but left them there in the bowl on his desk. He had not returned our call. He would not listen to our pleas, or if he listened, he would not be persuaded. Tessa would not survive. We gave up hope and adjusted ourselves. We stood by her bed as she continued in her coma. She only seemed asleep. We told her she was loved. We talked quietly as though fearing we would wake her. Clare was with us. In the dark of the room that night, Tessa passed quickly from us. Grace sat on the other side of her bed, her head bowed on the white sheet over Tessa's hand. It was as if Tessa couldn't wait to leave and was gone before she died. I felt she had seen something we didn't. Who knows who was with her then? My parents, Grace's grandparents, the angels, and God himself? It didn't matter that she was leaving earth. It didn't matter she would not be a bride. She would not have children. She would not be with us in the house to share our lives. It only mattered that she had a place to rise.

At Tessa's death, Grace's grief came in sobs. She was an open space into which she sucked air—in and out, in and out. Her family wanted to comfort her, but I told them to let her grieve. The nurses came into the room, but I raised my hand for them not to bother us. I had not heard Grace cry in that way. I let her cry the sounds I had not heard from her. Over and over until they diminished. She was emptied of tears for that night, but the heaving of breath continued, as would the tears in the days to come. Maybe I had not understood how Tessa's death had affected her. Maybe not Clare either, except for the resilience at her sister's death. What an open hole Tessa had left in our lives.

What was reason for Tessa's death? "That I might know him and the power of his resurrection," someone wrote. "That I might grow in the strength and grace of our Lord Jesus Christ," another pastor wrote. It angered me at first—that someone who had not been through what I had tried to comfort me.

Tessa's death was a walnut in my throat. I could suffer desolation and yet praise God as the absolute. He was more enormous than depression. Than death. Than the death of this depression. Could I have known this without being broken down? Could I have learned another way?

I was still dealing with Tessa's death, but Grace, Clare, and I would deal with it the rest of our lives. Now I had Thomas Fout. Had I failed him too? What could I have said that would stand up to the addiction to murder he had let himself develop? We all were alone. I was alone with myself. I had to read Scripture. I had to hold onto the faith that God was in control and I was resting under the shadow of his wings. I felt a small thrust of energy. I got up from the floor of my closet. I returned to the chair in my office. I felt overcome, yet I went on.

94

Zelda Gheary
City of Refuge

I continued with my *subworld* drawings. They were my city of refuge. They were the sturdy architecture I felt in church sanctuaries. I knew Ralph didn't understand. I kept the door locked, and he didn't ask for the key again. At times, I was fearful of Ralph. I mean, I saw his distrust. Was he talking to Mark Cabot about me? Had he called my parents? Had he gone to others? Would he come with someone and have me institutionalized? It was a possibility I considered. Sometimes I was afraid someone I didn't know would knock on the door. The *subworld* drawings continued across the ceiling of my workroom.

We were supposed to have people over to dinner—members of the congregation who were still struggling to understand what had happened. How could I help when I could not understand a God who let a murderer rip through our lives? It was Mark's idea, meant to help soothe the congregation. To have "dialogue," a word I hated. I mean, could anyone have dialogue with a God who put a plunderer in our congregation? Why didn't the Cabots have us to their house to soothe us?

During the day, I sat in the bungalow. In the evenings, Ralph and I hardly talked. We took our walk, then read or watched the news. Maybe someone was dying and Ralph had to make a run to the hospital. One evening when he was gone, I sat on my grandmother's old leather sofa and pulled her afghan over my feet and legs. Thomas Fout would always be connected to my grandmother's death because his arrest interrupted her funeral. I drew in my sketchbook openly, not hiding in my workroom. I drew the swirl of the Milky Way. The swirl of hell, which was the swirl of the self enlarged. I drew the swirl of Christ on the cross—marred beyond recognition. My *subworld* was alive, moving with terrifying images. Christ suffered the sins of humanity on the cross. Hatred. Murder. Torture. Black swirling tornados ate their way into his body. Somewhere, steel knives raked against metal bars with enormous clatter. Thomas Fout was in the center, clinging terrified to Christ. Christ's arm was around him. Others were beyond the reach of his salvation. They'd turned their backs, ignored him. Put him off. They were still horrified of him—a huge, dark, writhing worm on the cross. I drew in a sweat and kicked off the afghan. I saw the world outside God. I wrote words for Thomas Fout: "I made my world. I tasted my kingdom. I had a rider now." A great excitement was there for him: *All the world is coming. There is something to plot. To plan.* Could he erase it if he tried? Did he even want to? Look at the serpent not slithering now, but on its feet. My *subworld* was black and white, but I felt the serpent flame from the words I wrote. That's what art did for me. My *subworld* drawings showed me the world without Christ. That's why it took such a horrible death on the cross to atone for. My *subworld* drawings became the reminder that art was nothing beside God.

In my drawings, I restored feet to the serpent—feet that Thomas Fout taught me to draw: "You saw no manner of similitude on the day the Lord spoke to you—lest you make a graven image—lest you set yourself up as God."[1] "There was a God who drove out nations mightier than his own people and gave them their land for an inheritance."[2] I had the land of the demons for my inheritance. Because of Christ, I could go into my *subworld* and find my way back.

---

1. Deut 4:15.
2. Deut 4:38.

95

Mark Cabot
But for the Accident

The church voted to give me a sabbatical. Grace and I would stay in Buckholt. Clare was in school. We didn't want to move her again. Roy and Beth Saith offered to keep her, and she wanted to stay with them. Claire actually seemed disappointed when we declined the offer. But I didn't know where else to go. I would work in my office. Maybe I would write articles on my experience. Roy said I could spend as much time at Lake Orbson as I wanted, but there had been so much construction, it wasn't the same lake.

Had all my years of faithfulness come to this? I held on through my submarine ride. It had separated me from myself. I saw the hardening of my wife and could do nothing about it. Eventually, other events would happen that would pull public attention away from Thomas Fout and Christ Church in Buckholt, Kansas. Just give it time.

I felt I had discovered an unspeakable knowledge hidden below the surface of everyday, ordinary life. Again, I wept bitterly behind the door of the closet of my church office. I waited for time to pass. For people to stop staring. Maybe in fifty years I could shop and no one would recognize me. I could pass unnoticed. I could think the people in the car next to me at a stoplight were staring. It would be possible to go through a day without thinking about Thomas Fout. No, he would always be there, even if he were dead. That one thing I knew.

One of Us

There were Biblical passages I had puzzled over. Then suddenly they were clear, or at least, seemed clear at the moment. Michael, the archangel, when contending with the devil about the body of Moses, dared not bring against him a railing accusation, but said, "The Lord rebuke you."[1] Did they argue because Moses had murdered? And a murderer could to go to heaven?

At least it was what the verse meant to me in this particular circumstance. "And he showed me Joshua, the high priest, standing before the angel of the Lord, and Satan standing at his right hand to resist him. And the Lord said to Satan, The Lord rebuke you, Satan."[2]

"The Lord rebuke you," I said in front of Thomas Fout at Wyatt.

That was the brunt of my exorcism. How watered down it seemed.

I had been crucified to my ability to cope with anything. I found I could do nothing in the face of evil. I was flattened to the ground. What would come of it? What effect would it have? Would my experience be like Job's? Would I know God in a different way than I did? We come before you, Lord. We are the broken. We are the overburdened. Restore us again. None of us were the same after contact with sin and the knowledge of evil.

There was an accident ahead on the interstate as I returned from Wyatt. I stopped in a long line of cars. I prayed for those ahead. An hour later, traffic had barely moved. I saw the highway patrol directing traffic off the interstate to a narrow road that led west to another highway. I called Grace and told her I would be late. Traffic crept on the road. I thought of truckers on a time schedule.

It had turned cold early in the winter. The sky was gray. I rolled down the window on the passenger's side and looked out across the Kansas fields. The stubbled rows held a few narrow ribbons of old snow. Several broken stalks stood at a right angle bent down to the ground, almost like crosses on their sides. Wherever I was, I knew he was one of us too.

As I sat there, it started to snow. I watched a few large flakes swirling in the air. I saw the row of trees in the distance. Windbreaks, they were called. A few flurries danced into the open window of the car. I put my hand out to them. They seemed to circle before me, drawing me to them. They had

---

1. Jude 9.
2. Zech 3:1–2.

fallen from the sky—here on the road—where I would not have been but for an accident.

www.ingramcontent.com/pod-product-compliance
Lightning Source LLC
Chambersburg PA
CBHW062022220426
43662CB00010B/1428